TOTAL
CROCHET
for the home

Produced for Leisure Arts by MQ Publications Limited
MQ Publications New York office:
49 West 24th Street, 8th floor
New York, NY 10010
Phone: (+1) 212 223 6342
London office:
12 The Ivories
6–8 Northampton Street
London N1 2HY
Phone: + 44 (0)20 7359 2244
Website: www.mqpublications.com

Publisher and CEO: Zaro Weil
Group Sales Director: Simon Majumdar
Vice President of Sales and Marketing, North America: Stacey Ashton
Editorial Director: Ljiljana Baird
Editor: Sorrel Wood
Developmental Editor: BJ Berti
Technical Editor: Mari Lynn Patrick
Photography on pages 4–63: Vincent Scilla
Photography on pages 64–109: Lizzie Orme
Design: Joanna Hill, Redbox Design

TOTAL
CROCHET
for the home

BJ BERTI

contents

THE PROJECTS

introduction

There's nothing like handmade textiles to give a home warmth, comfort, and a sense of personal style. And there's no easier way to create your own fine pieces than with a crochet hook and a ball of yarn.

Newcomers to crochet will find some very pleasant surprises in these pages—among them, how quickly some of the projects can be completed. And I hope that even lifelong crocheters will find inspiration in the yarn and color choices, and in the ease with which this age-old craft adapts to contemporary decorating styles—whether your preference is traditional, eclectic, or high-tech modern.

The art of crochet dates back so far, its precise origins continue to elude scholars. But we are all familiar with the doilies, antimacassars, blankets, throws, and lacy tablecloths our grandmothers and great-grandmothers proudly displayed. As you approach this book, however, I'd like you to forget those old family pieces—at least briefly—because in recent years, this traditional craft has been transformed. In these pages, you'll discover the new crochet, revitalized with new materials and new designs for a clean, contemporary look. Even the classic projects I've included such as the tea cozy, pot holders, and afghans are designed to work beautifully in the 21st century home.

These projects take advantage of the gold mine of yarns available nowadays, from plushy to delicate, in a broad palette of fresh, dynamic colors. The accents these projects bring to a room may be subtle or dramatic, but they are all practical and pretty, designed to contribute stunning spots of color, texture, or an airy touch of lace to soften or contrast with hard edges.

For the novice crocheter, several of the projects offer instant gratification. Even if you're picking up a crochet hook for the first time, you can work the pot holders or lacy pillow trims quickly and easily. Just turn to page 90, and you'll find all the basic stitch techniques, tips, and information you will need to get started. Crochet aficionados may want to start straightaway on some of the table decorations, bags, or dresser-top pots.

Versatility is one of the hallmarks of crochet. If you've never made an afghan before, you'll be amazed to see how portable your work can be. A granny square in progress goes anywhere, even in your sleekest handbag. Just bring along your sense of whimsy and adventure, and discover how accessories you can make in a few short hours will bring a fresh look to every room of your home.

chunky pillows

Throw one on a chair, arrange a pair on a couch or bed, or better still, use all three of these versatile pillows together for a splash of texture and color. Each pillow is worked in a simple pattern designed to both blend and contrast with its mates.

FINISHED MEASUREMENTS

- Olive pillow 18" x 18" (46 cm x 46 cm)
- Pumpkin pillow 18" x 18" (46 cm x 46 cm)
- Spice pillow 16" x 16" (40.5 cm x 40.5 cm)

MATERIALS

 8 x 3½ oz. (100 g) balls, each approx. 60 yd. (54 m) long, of Tahki Stacy Charles *Baby* (wool) in #22 Olive
- 8 x 3½ oz. (100 g) balls, each approx. 60 yd. (54 m) long, of Tahki Stacy Charles *Baby* (wool) in #8 Pumpkin
- 3 x 6 oz (170 g) balls, each approx. 106 yd. (97 m) long, of Lion Brand *Wool-Ease Thick & Quick* (acrylic/wool) in #135 Spice
- Size K-10½ (6.5 mm) crochet hook, OR SIZE NECESSARY TO OBTAIN CORRECT GAUGE
- Tapestry needle for seams
- 2 x 18" (46 cm) pillow forms
- 1 x 16" (40.5 cm) pillow form

GAUGE

OLIVE PILLOW

10 sts and 6 rows = 4" (10 cm) in pattern st.

PUMPKIN PILLOW

11 sts = 5" (12.5 cm).

6 rows = 4" (10 cm) in pattern st.

SPICE PILLOW

10 sts and 6 rows = 4" (10 cm) in pattern st.

BE SURE TO CHECK THE GAUGE.

STITCH GLOSSARY

Dc dec [yo, pull up loop in next st, yo and through 2 loops] twice, yo and through 3 loops.

Front Post St (FPS) Yo, insert hook from front to back to front around post of st below, yo, pull up a loop, yo and complete as dc.

Back Post St (BPS) Yo, insert hook from back to front to back around post of st below, yo, pull up a loop, yo and complete as dc.

PATTERN A

Row 1 (RS) Hdc in first st, [hdc in back loop of 4 sts, FPS over next 4 sts] across, hdc in last st. Ch 2, turn.

Row 2 (WS) Hdc in first st; [BPS over next 4 sts, hdc in front loop of 4 sts] across, hdc in last st. Ch 2, turn.

Row 3 Hdc in first st, [FPS over next 4 sts, hdc in back loop of 4 sts] across, hdc in last st. Ch 2, turn.

Row 4 Hdc in first st, [hdc in front loop 4 of sts, BPS over next 4 sts] across, hdc in last st. Ch 2, turn.

PATTERN B

Row 1 (RS) Hdc in back loop of first st; [hdc in back loop of 3 sts, FPS around next st] across, end hdc in back loop of last 4 sts. Ch 2, turn.

Row 2 (WS) Hdc in front loop of first st, [hdc in front loop of 3 sts, BPS around next st] across, end hdc in front loop of last 4 sts. Ch 2, turn.

Pumpkin pillow

side a

Ch 44; dc in 3rd ch from hook and in each ch across—42 sts. Rep 4 rows of pat A until piece measures 18" (46 cm). Fasten off.

side b

Ch 44; dc in 3rd ch from hook and in each ch across—42 sts. Rep rows 1 and 2 of pat B until piece measures 18" (46 cm). Fasten off.

finishing

With WS tog, sew side seams on 3 sides. Insert pillow form. Sew rem side.

Olive pillow

front and back (make 2 alike)

Ch 42, dc in 3rd ch from hook and in each ch across—40 dc. Ch 3, turn.
Row 1 Working in back loops only, dc in base of ch 3; ★ dc in next 2 sts; [dc dec over next 2 sts] twice; dc in next 2 sts, [2 dc in next st] twice; rep from ★ across, ending last rep with 2 dc in last st. Ch 3, turn.
Rep row 1 until piece measures 18" (46 cm). Fasten off.

finishing

With WS tog, sew side seams on 3 sides. Insert pillow form. Sew rem side.

Spice pillow

front and back (make 2 alike)

Ch 38, hdc in 2nd ch from hook and in each ch across—37 hdc. Ch 2, turn.
Row 1 [Hdc in back loop of next st, hdc in front loop of next st] across; hdc in back loop of last st. Rep row 1 until piece measures 16" (40.5 cm). Fasten off.

finishing

With WS tog, sew side seams on 3 sides. Insert pillow form. Sew rem side.

star pattern afghan

Admiring eyes will be drawn to the striking colors of this dramatic coverlet. The central pattern is worked in two shades of plum. The darker shade is repeated in the open border of muted green-gray, dark purple, and brown. A great way to keep warm on a chill summer evening or a midwinter night by the fire.

FINISHED MEASUREMENTS

- Width approx. 43" (109 cm)
- Length approx. 55" (140 cm)
- Border width 3½" (9 cm)

MATERIALS

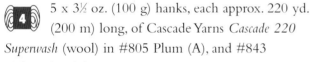 5 x 3½ oz. (100 g) hanks, each approx. 220 yd. (200 m) long, of Cascade Yarns *Cascade 220 Superwash* (wool) in #805 Plum (A), and #843 Light Wine (B)
- 1 x 3½ oz. (100 g) hank, approx. 220 yd. (200 m) long, of Cascade Yarns *Cascade 220 Superwash* (wool) in #803 Dark Purple (C), #818 Brown (D), and #816 Gray (E)
- Size H-8 (5 mm) crochet hook, OR SIZE NECCESSARY TO OBTAIN CORRECT GAUGE

GAUGE

2 Star patterns = 3½" (9 cm). BE SURE TO CHECK THE GAUGE.

STITCH GLOSSARY

Unfin dc Yo, pull up loop in indicated st, yo and through 2 loops only.
Shell [3 dc, ch 2, 3 dc] in one sp.
Small shell [2 dc, ch 2, 2 dc] in one sp.

Afghan

With A, ch 165. Sc in 2nd ch from hook and in each ch across—164 sc. Ch 1, turn.
Row 1 ★ Sc in first sc; [skip 2 sts, 7 dc in next st, skip 2 sts, sc in next st] across. Drop A; attach B.
Row 2 With B, ch 3, unfin dc in next 3 dc; yo and through 4 loops. ★ Ch 4, sc in center dc of 7-dc group, ch 3, unfin dc in 3 dc, unfin dc in sc, unfin dc in next 3 dc, yo and through all 8 loops (Star Group made); rep from ★ across row, ending with unfin dc in last 3 dc, unfin dc in last sc, yo and through 5 loops. Ch 3, turn.
Row 3 3 dc into base of ch-3; [sc in sc, 7 dc in closing st of row 2] across, ending with 4 dc in last sc. Drop B, pick up A. Ch 1, turn.
Row 4 Sc in dc, [ch 3, Star Group over next 7 sts, ch 4, sc in center dc of 7-dc group] across; sc in last st. Ch 1, turn.
Row 5 Sc in first st, [7 dc in closing st of previous row, sc in next sc] across. Drop A, pick up B.
Rep rows 2–5 for pattern until piece measures 55" (140 cm), ending with row 4 (A).

border

Rnd 1 With A, sc evenly around 4 sides, working 3 sc in each corner. Join with Sl st to first sc. Fasten off.
Rnd 2 With D, join and ch 3, (counts as dc), dc in next 2 sts; ★ [ch 3, skip 3 sts, dc in next 3 sts] to corner ★★; ch 4 for corner; dc in next 3 sts; rep

from ★ twice; rep from ★ to ★★ once. Ch 2, hdc in top of ch 3 to join.

NOTE Be certain that corresponding sides have the same number of 3-dc groups. Do not turn.

Rnd 3 Ch 3, 2 dc in sp created by hdc; [ch 3, skip 3 dc; 3 dc in next ch-3 sp] around, working [3 dc, ch 3, 3 dc] in each corner sp, and ending with [3 dc in corner sp; ch 3; Sl st in top of ch-3 to join]. Fasten off D.

Rnd 4 Attach A in any corner sp; ch 1, sc in same sp; ★ [ch 3, skip 3-dc group; shell in next ch-3 sp; ch 3, skip 3-dc group, sc in next ch-3 sp] to corner; making any necessary adjustments to end with [sc, ch 1, sc] in ch-3 corner sp; rep from ★ around. Sl st in beg sc to join. Fasten off A.

Rnd 5 Attach E in any corner sp, ch 3 (for dc) [ch 1, dc] 5 times all in same sp, skipping all ch-3s, ★ [ch 1, dc] 6 times in ch-2 sp of shell; ch 1, small shell in next sc; rep from ★ around. Join in top of ch-3; fasten off E.

Rnd 6 Join C in any corner ch-2 sp, ch 3, dc, ch 1, dc in same sp, ★ [ch 1, dc in next ch-1 sp] twice, ch 1, dc in ch-1 sp, sc in center ch-2 sp of small shell, dc in next ch-1 sp, [ch 1, dc in next ch-1 sp] twice, [ch 1, dc in next ch-1 sp] 3 times all into same sp; rep from ★ around. Join and fasten off.

latticework place mat
and napkin ring

Just right for casual entertaining or family meals, these washable mats will grace your table with flair. Choose matching or contrasting colors for the buttoned-up napkin rings and, when it's time to select the buttons, let your imagination reign for an effect that can be subtle, bold, or anything in between.

FINISHED MEASUREMENTS

- Place mat 11½" x 17½" (29 cm x 44.5 cm)
- Napkin ring 1¾" x 6" (4.5 cm x 15.3 cm)

MATERIALS

 3 x 1 oz. (29 g) balls, each approx. 100 yd. (91 m) long, of DMC *Senso 730 U* (wool/cotton) in #1304 Olive Green (makes 1 place mat and napkin ring)
- Size F-4 (3.5 mm) crochet hook, OR SIZE NECESSARY TO OBTAIN CORRECT GAUGE
- 2 x ½" (1.5 cm) buttons for each napkin ring

GAUGE

4 patterns = 5" (12.5 cm)
3 rows of the pattern = 4" (10 cm). BE SURE TO CHECK THE GAUGE.

NOTE Yarn is used double throughout.

LATTICE STITCH

Row 1 (WS) Ch 6, [skip 3 hdc, sc into hdc; ch 2, tr in dc, ch 2] across; tr in top of turning ch.
Row 2 Ch 6 (counts as dc, ch 3); [sc in sc, ch 2, turn work, 4 hdc into ch 3 sp; ch 2, turn work; hdc in back loop of each hdc; dc in next tr] across, with last dc in 3rd ch of ch 6.

Place mat

With a double strand of yarn, ch 78 sts.
Foundation row Sc in 9th ch from hook (counts as dc, ch 3); ch 2, turn; 4 hdc into ch-3 sp; turn, hdc into back loop of 4 hdc, (block made); skip 2 ch of starting ch; dc in next ch; ★ ch 3, skip 2 ch, sc in next ch; ch 2, turn; 4 hdc into ch-3 sp; turn, hdc into back loop of 4 hdc; (block made); skip 2 ch of starting ch; dc in next ch; rep from ★ across, ending with dc in last ch.
Beg with row 1 of lattice stitch; rep rows 1 and 2 until piece measures 11" (28 cm) from beg, ending with row 1. Ch 1, turn. Sc evenly across top, down end, across bottom and back to beg, working 3 sc at each corner. Fasten off.

end

With WS facing, hdc in each sc across end.
Ch 2, turn.
Row 1 Hdc in back loop of each hdc across.
Ch 2, turn.

> **style tip** If you make a set of six place mats and napkin rings for a dinner party, make two extra mats for the center of the table to serve from.

Row 2 Hdc in front loop of each hdc across. Ch 2, turn.

Rep rows 1 and 2 until end measures 1" (2.5 cm) from beg; ending with row 2. Ch 1, turn.

Next row Sc in back loop of each hdc across. Fasten off. Rep for other end.

finishing

Attach yarn in any corner; sc in each sc around, working 3 sc at each corner. Fasten off.

Napkin ring

With double strand of yarn; ch 27. Hdc in 2nd ch from hook and in each ch across. Ch 2, turn. Rep row 1 and row 2 of instructions for end. Ch 1, turn; sc in back loop of each hdc across.

Ch 1, working along top, down end, across bottom, and up other end, sc evenly around. Fasten off.

finishing

Sew 2 small buttons on one short end; button through hdc sp at other end.

zigzag **tea cozy**

While your brew is steeping, keep it warm in traditional style. Once an indispensable accessory for the well-appointed home, the energy-efficient cozy is making a comeback. With smart stripes and a sleek fit, our design will find a comfy spot in any kitchen. And it's almost as simple to make as a cup of tea.

MATERIALS

 2 x 3½ oz. (100 g) balls, each approx. 186 yd. (170 m) long, of TLC *Cotton Plus*, (cotton/acrylic) in #3811 Medium Blue (A)

● 1 x 3½ oz. (100 g) ball, approx. 186 yd. (170 m) long, of TLC *Cotton Plus*, (cotton/acrylic) in #3643 Kiwi (B), #3001 White (C), #3810 Light Blue (D), and #3252 Tangerine (E)

● Size F-5 (3.75 mm) crochet hook, OR SIZE NECESSARY TO OBTAIN CORRECT GAUGE

GAUGE

18 sc and 16 rows = 4" (10 cm). BE SURE TO CHECK THE GAUGE.

STITCH GLOSSARY

Hdc Dec [Yo, pull up loop in next st] twice; yo and through all loops on hook.
Sc Dec [Pull up loop in next st] twice, yo and through all loops on hook.

RIPPLE PATTERN

Row 1 ★ 2 hdc in next st; hdc in next st, [hdc dec over next 2 sts] twice, hdc in next st, 2 hdc in next st; rep from ★ across.

NOTE Entire cozy is worked on RS rows in back loops only; on WS rows in front loops only. Carry all colors loosely along the sides of the piece and bring up to work new color in stripe pat.

Cozy

body side (make 2)

With A, ch 42.
Row 1 (RS) With A, sc in 2nd ch from hook and in each ch across—41 sts; drop A. With B, ch 1, turn.
Row 2 (WS) With B, sc in front loop of each st. Drop B; with C, ch 1, turn.
Row 3 With C, sc in back loop of each st. Drop C; with D, ch 1, turn.
Row 4 With D, sc in front loop of each st. Drop D; with E, ch 1, turn.
Row 5 With E, sc in back loop of each st. Drop E; with A, ch 1, turn.
Row 6 With A, sc in front loop of each st. Drop A; with B, ch 1, turn.
Row 7 With B, sc in back loop of each st. Drop B; with C, ch 1, turn.
Row 8 With C, sc in front loop of each st. Drop C; with D, ch 2, turn.
Row 9 With D, working in back loops only, hdc in base of ch-2, hdc in next st, [hdc dec over 2 sts] twice, hdc in next st, 2 hdc in next st, rep from ★ of row 1 of ripple pat across. Pick up E; ch 2, turn.
Row 10 With E, rep row 9, working in front loops only. Pick up C.
Row 11 With C, rep row 9, working in back loops only. Pick up B.
Row 12 With B, rep row 9, working in front loops only. Pick up A.

EDGING

With WS tog, attach A in lower left corner of side 1. Inserting hook through edges of side 1 and 2 at the same time, and working from left to right, work backwards sc through both thicknesses around the shaped sides, then cont through single thickness only across the lower open edge. Fasten off.

HANGER

Attach A in center edge of top, ch 11, Sl st in base of ch to form a large loop, ch 1, turn. Sc 22 times in loop; Sl st to cozy to join. Fasten off.

Row 13 With A, rep row 9, working in back loops only. Pick up D.

Row 14 With D, rep row 9, working in front loops only. Pick up E.

Row 15 Rep row 5.

Row 16 With A, rep row 6.

Row 17 With B, rep row 7, dec sc at beg and end of row.

Row 18 With C, rep row 8, dec sc at beg and end of row.

Row 19 With D, rep row 3, dec sc at beg and end of row.

Row 20 With E, rep row 4, dec sc at beg and end of row.

Row 21–26 Rep rows 1–6, changing colors and dec sc at beg and end of each row. Fasten off.

finishing

Attach A in any corner of side 1, ch 1, sc in same st with joining, sc evenly around, working [sc, ch 2, sc] in each lower corner. Rep for side 2.

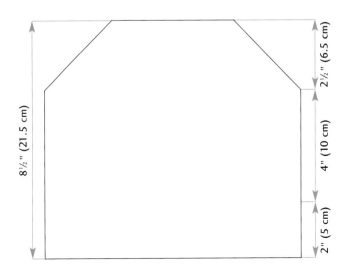

multistripe **tote**

Chunky yarn worked sideways in stripes makes this carryall bag fun to create. The wide strap is attached afterward using blanket stitch and contrast color yarn. The bag can also be lined, if desired, for additional support.

FINISHED MEASUREMENTS
- Width 16" (40.5 cm)
- Height 14" (35.5 cm)

MATERIALS
1 x 5 oz. (140 g) ball, approx. 153 yd (140 m) long, of Lion Brand *Wool-Ease Chunky* (acrylic/wool) in #140 Deep Rose (A), #107 Blue Bell (B), #146 Orchid (C), #178 Nantucket (D), and #133 Pumpkin (E)
- Size K-10½ (6.5 mm) crochet hook, OR SIZE NECESSARY TO OBTAIN CORRECT GAUGE
- Tapestry needle

GAUGE
12 sts and 11 rows = 4" (10 cm) in pattern st.
BE SURE TO CHECK THE GAUGE.

STRIPE SEQUENCE
Front and back—rep sequence twice for each side.
½" (1 cm) A: Deep Rose (approx. 1 row)
2" (5 cm) B: Bluebell (approx. 5 rows)
1" (2.5 cm) C: Orchid (approx. 3 rows)
1" (2.5 cm) D: Nantucket (approx. 3 rows)
½" (1 cm) E: Pumpkin (approx. 2 rows)
1" (2.5 cm) A: Deep Rose (approx. 3 rows)
2" (5 cm) B: Bluebell (approx. 5 rows)

Bag

front and back (make 2 pieces alike)
With A, ch 42. Sc in 2nd ch from hook and in each ch across—41 sc. Ch 1, turn.
Row 1 (RS) With color B from stripe sequence, working in back loops only, sc in each sc across. Ch 1, turn.
Row 2 (WS) With color from stripe sequence, working in front loops only, sc in each sc across. Ch 1, turn.
Work 2 repeats of the stripe sequence, until piece measures 16" (40.5 cm) or desired length from beg.

strap
With C, ch 9, sc in 2nd ch from hook and in each ch to end. Ch 1, turn—8 sc.
Work even on 8 sc for 4 rows C, 5 rows A, 11 rows D, 12 rows E, 9 rows C, 6 rows B, 4 rows A, 13 rows D, 6 rows C, 4 rows E, 5 rows A, 6 rows B, 7 rows A. Fasten off.

finishing
Sc bag tog from WS along the sides and lower edges. With B, sc evenly around top; join in beg st ch 1, do not turn. Working from left to right, work backwards sc in each sc around top. Fasten off. Overlap strap by 4" (10 cm) along the side edges. Using buttonhole st and A, sew strap ends securely in place, as shown in the photo.

vintage pot holders

Re-create the beauty and subtlety of heirloom handwork in shades of blue and white. Practical as well as decorative, these pot holders are fun to make and a great addition to any kitchen—and perfect to give away as gifts.

FINISHED MEASUREMENTS

● 6½" (16.5 cm)

MATERIALS

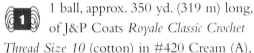 1 ball, approx. 350 yd. (319 m) long, of J&P Coats *Royale Classic Crochet Thread Size 10* (cotton) in #420 Cream (A), and #480 Delft (B)

● Size C-2 (2.75 mm) crochet hook, OR SIZE NECESSARY TO OBTAIN CORRECT GAUGE

GAUGE

8 dc and 10 rows = 4" (10 cm) over dc pat. BE SURE TO CHECK THE GAUGE.

STITCH GLOSSARY

Picot Ch 3, Sl st in first ch.

NOTE Thread is used as a double strand throughout. Each pot holder consists of 2 identical pieces for a double thickness when finished.

Striped pot holder (make 2)

NOTE Entire holder is worked in back loops only. With 2 strands of Color B held together, ch 5; Sl st to first ch to form a ring.

Rnd 1 (RS) Ch 3 (counts as dc), 17 dc in ring; Sl st in top of ch 3—18 dc.

Rnd 2 Working in back loops only, ch 3 (counts as dc); dc in same st; ★ dc in next st, 2 dc in next st, ch 2 ★★, 2 dc in next st; rep from ★ 4 times, rep from ★ to ★★ once. Sl st in top of ch 3 to join at end of this and every rnd.

Rnd 3 Ch 3 (counts as dc), dc in same st; ★ dc in next 3 sts, 2 dc in next st; ch 2, skip the ch 2 ★★, 2 dc in next dc; rep from ★ 4 times, rep from ★ to ★★ once. Join. Fasten off B; attach A.

Rnd 4 With A, ch 3 (counts as dc), dc in same st; ★ dc in next 5 sts, 2 dc in next st; ch 2, skip the ch 2 ★★, 2 dc in next dc; rep from ★ 4 times, rep from ★ to ★★ once. Join.

Rnd 5 Ch 3 (counts as dc), dc in same st; ★ dc in next 7 sts, 2 dc in next st; ch 2, skip the ch 2 ★★, 2 dc in next dc; rep from ★ 4 times, rep from ★ to ★★ once. Join. Fasten off A; attach B.

Rnds 6 and 7 With B, work as for rnd 5, having 2 additional dc in each section on every row—15 dc in each section at end of row 7. Fasten off A; attach B.

Rnd 8 With B, ch 4 (for dc, ch 1), ★ skip 1 st, [dc, ch 1] in next st; rep from ★ to ch-2 sp; in ch-2 sp work [dc, ch 1, dc, ch 1] ★★, dc in next dc. Rep from ★ 4 times, then from ★ to ★★ once; join.

NOTE Make a 2nd piece of holder 1 before cont.
Finishing Rnd 9 Working through both thicknesses
to join pieces, Sl st into next ch–1 sp; ch 1, sc in
same sp; ★ [hdc, dc, picot, dc, hdc] in next ch–1 sp;
skip dc, sc in next ch–1 sp, skip dc; rep from ★
around. Join in Sl st. Fasten off.

finishing

HANGER LOOP

With double strand of A, join at back of pot holder in one ch-1 sp, ch 8, join in same space.
Into ch-8 loop work ch 1, 5 sc, picot, 5 sc.
Fasten off.

Square pot holder (make 2)

With 2 strands of B, ch 37. Dc in 4th ch from hook, dc in next 3 ch, [ch 1, skip 1 ch, dc in 5 ch] 5 times. Ch 3, turn.
Row 1 Dc in 2nd st and next 3 dc, [ch 1, skip 1 ch, dc in 5 dc] 5 times. Turn.
Row 2 Ch 3 (counts as hdc, ch 1); [ch 1, skip 1 st, hdc in next st, ch 1] across, ending last rep with hdc in last st. Ch 3, turn.
Row 3 Rep row 1.
Rep rows 1–3 until piece measures 5½" (14 cm) from beg, ending with row 2—18 hdc across. Ch 3, do not turn.
Turning pot holder and working down side, across bottom, and up other side, with ch 3 at each corner, [hdc in row or sp, ch 1] around, making adjustments to have 18 hdc on each side. Fasten off. Make 2 pieces before finishing.

finishing

With WS tog, attach A in any corner, working through both sides at once, ch 2, [2 hdc in each ch-1 sp] around, working 5 hdc in each corner ch-3 sp. Sl st in top of ch 2. Turn.

HANGER LOOP

Ch 8, Sl st in corner sp to form a large loop, ch 1, turn. Sc 12 times in loop; Sl st to potholder to join. Fasten off.

Tweedy pot holder (make 2)

With 2 strands of B, ch 10; Sl st in first ch to form a ring. Work 22 sc into ring; Sl st to join. Drop 1 strand of B; attach 1 strand of A.
Row 1 Working with 1 strand each of A and B, ch 3 (counts as dc), dc into next 5 sc in ring, ch 2 (for center), dc into next 6 sc. Ch 3, turn.
Row 2 Dc in each dc to center, [2 dc, ch 2, 2 dc] in center ch-2 sp; dc to end. Ch 3, turn.
[Rep row 2] 10 times more. Drop A, attach 1 strand B.
Make 2 pieces before finishing.

finishing

BORDER

With WS tog, using 2 strands of B, and working through both sides at once, [sc in next dc, skip 2 dc, 5 dc in next dc, sk 2 sts] down 1 side, in corner, and around other side. Fasten off.

style tip Work a second pot holder in each pattern, but reverse the colorways to make a stylish set.

summer farm **afghan**

Shades of green and maize combine in tricolor blocks joined with an openwork stitch. A wide openwork border in the same alternating colors forms a lacy frame around the blocks. The block works well in two shades of the same color. Remember that the colors can be changed to reflect the decor of your home.

FINISHED MEASUREMENTS

- Width approx. 50" (127 cm), including border
- Length approx. 58" (147 cm), including border

MATERIALS

5 x 3½ oz. (100 g) skeins, each approx. 223 yd. (205 m) long, of Patons *Classic Merino Wool* (wool) in #0252 Tree Bark Mix (A), and #0203 Maize (C)
- 3 x 3½ oz. (100 g) skeins, each approx. 223 yd. (205 m) long, of Patons *Classic Merino Wool* (wool) in #0240 Leaf Green (B)
- Size H-8 (5 mm) crochet hook, OR SIZE NECESSARY TO OBTAIN CORRECT GAUGE

GAUGE

Motif = 7¼" (18.5 cm) across. BE SURE TO CHECK THE GAUGE.

CLUSTER PATTERN

Holding last loops on hook, ★ Yo twice, pull up loop in next st; [yo and through 2 loops] twice; rep from ★ 3 times, yo and through all loops on hook.

Afghan

motif (make 42)

With A, ch 8, Sl st to first ch to form a ring.

Rnd 1 (RS) With A, ch 4 (counts as tr), 5 tr in ring; [ch 3, 6 tr in ring] 3 times; ch 3; Sl st to top of ch-4.

Rnd 2 ★ Ch 5 (counts as tr), cluster over 4 sts; ch 5, Sl st in next tr (large cluster made); ch 1, Sl st in ch-3 sp; rep from ★ 3 times—4 large clusters. Fasten off A.

Rnd 3 Join B to top of any large cluster; work ★ [3 tr, ch 1, 3 tr, ch 2 for corner, 3 tr, ch 1, 3 tr] in ch-3 sp of rnd 1, Sl st in top of next large cluster; rep from ★ 3 times. Sl st in joining. Fasten off B.

Rnd 4 Join A in ch-1 sp of rnd 3 (to right of large cluster), ch 1, Sl st in same st; ★ 6 tr in Sl st of rnd 3; Sl st in ch-1 sp; [6 tr, ch 2, 6 tr] in next corner; Sl st in ch-1 sp; rep from ★ 3 times; Sl st to ch-1 at joining. Fasten off A.

Rnd 5 Join C in last Sl st of rnd 4; ch 1, ★ sc in next 6 tr; dc over Sl st into ch-1 sp of rnd 3; sc in next 6 tr, 3 sc in ch-2 corner sp, sc in next 6 tr, dc over sl sl into ch-1 sp of rnd 3. Rep from ★ 3 times; Sl st in joining.

Rnd 6 With C, Sl st in first sc, ch 4 (counts as dc, ch 1), skip 1 st, dc in 3rd sc, ch 1, skip 1 st, ★ [dc in next st, ch 1, skip 1 st] 5 times, dc in next st, ch 1, in 2nd sc of corner, work [dc, ch 1] 3 times; [dc in next st, ch 1, skip 1 st] 5 times, dc in next st, ch 1; rep from ★ 3 times, ending last rep with [dc in next st, ch 1, skip 1 st] 4 times, Sl st in 3rd ch of ch-4. Fasten off C.

finishing

Arrange motifs with 6 across and 7 lengthwise strips.

JOINING THE MOTIFS

With C, holding 2 motifs with WS tog, attach yarn in left-hand corner of front motif. Ch 1, inserting hook through ch-1 sps of both motifs, working from left to right, [sc in next ch-1 sp, ch 1, skip dc] across.

border

Rnd 1 Attach B in any ch-1 sp; ch 2 for hdc, hdc in same sp; [2 hdc in next ch-1 sp] around, working [2 hdc in ch-1 sp, ch 2, 2 hdc in next ch-1 sp] at corners. Fasten off.

Rnd 2 Attach A in any ch-2 corner sp; [ch 1, skip hdc, dc in next hdc] around, working [dc, ch 1] 3 times in each ch-2 corner. Fasten off A.

Rnd 3 Attach B in any center dc of corner; [ch 5, skip dc, sc in next dc] around. Sl st to beg to join.

Rnd 4 Sl st in ch-5; ★ [2 sc, ch 1, 2 sc] in next ch-5 sp, Sl st in sc; rep from ★ around. Fasten off B.

Rnd 5 Attach C in any ch-1 sp; [ch 5, sc in next ch-1 sp] around, substituting ch 7 for ch-5 in corners. Sl st to beg to join.

Rnd 6 Sl st into ch-5 sp; ch 1, sc in same sp. [Ch 1, 4 tr in next ch-5 sp, ch 1, sc in next ch-5 sp] around, making any adjustment to make corners lay flat. Fasten off.

openwork
table runner

Protect your sideboard, dresser, or dining table, and pretty up the room at the same time with this multitasking runner. It's the perfect foil for any centerpiece. Worked in a wool-and-cotton yarn that's easy to wash, the shell stitch creates the delicate feel that many think of as the essence of crochet.

FINISHED MEASUREMENTS
- Width 17" (43 cm)
- Length 55" (140 cm)

MATERIALS
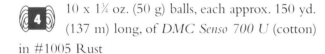 10 x 1¾ oz. (50 g) balls, each approx. 150 yd. (137 m) long, of *DMC Senso 700 U* (cotton) in #1005 Rust
- Size G-6 (4 mm) crochet hook, OR SIZE NECESSARY TO OBTAIN CORRECT GAUGE

GAUGE
1 Pattern = 3" (7.5 cm). BE SURE TO CHECK THE GAUGE.

NOTE Yarn is used double throughout.

style tip Try adding the border as a trim along the edges of pillows or seat cushions in the room you choose to display the table runner. Use a yarn that provides a contrast with the dominant colors of the room, without clashing with any strong colors.

Table runner

With a double strand of yarn, ch 72 sts.
Foundation row Sc in 2nd ch from hook; ★ ch 5, skip 3 ch, sc in next ch; rep from ★ to last 2 ch; ch 2, skip 1 ch, dc in last ch, turn.
Row 1 (RS) Ch 1, 1 sc in first st, skip ch-2 sp; ★ 7 dc in next ch-5 arch, sc in next ch-5 arch ★★, ch 5, sc in next arch; rep from ★ across, ending last rep at ★★; ch 2, tr in last sc; skip turning ch, turn.
Row 2 Ch 1, sc in first st; ★ ch 5, sc into 2nd dc of next 7–dc group, ch 5, sc into 6th dc of same group; ★★, ch 5, sc into next ch-5 arch; rep from ★ across, ending last rep at ★★; ch 2, tr into last sc; skip turning ch, turn.
Rep rows 1 and 2 until piece measures 49" (124.5 cm) or desired length, ending with row 1. Do not fasten off.

finishing
Ch 1, sc in same st; working down long side, sc evenly down side, across bottom and on rem sides, working 3 sc in each corner. Sl st in beg sc to join.
Row 2 Ch 1, sc in same st, sc in each sc around, working 3 sc at each corner. Fasten off.

border
With RS facing, attach the yarn in center sc of right corner.

Row 1 Ch 1, sc in same st; [ch 1, skip 1 st, sc in next st] across, making any adjustment to have 65 sts, turn.

Row 2 Sl st into first ch-1 sp; ch 5 (counts as dc, ch 2); dc in same st; ★ skip 3 ch-1 sps (7 sts), ch 3, [tr, ch 5, tr] into next ch-1 sp, ch 3, skip 3 ch-1 sps (7 sts), [dc, ch 2, dc] in next ch-1 sp, rep from ★ across, ending last rep in last st—(5 dc groups; 4 tr groups), turn.

Row 3 Ch 5 (counts as dc, ch 2), dc in base of ch-5; ★ [4 tr, ch 5, 4 tr] in ch-5 loop; [dc, ch 2, dc] in ch-2 sp; rep from ★ across. Turn.

Row 4 Ch 6 (counts as dc, ch 3), dc in base of ch-5; ★ [ch 1, tr] 9 times in ch-5 sp; ch 1, [2 dc, ch 2, 2 dc] in ch-2 sp; rep from ★ across, ending last rep with [dc, ch 2, dc] in last ch-2 sp. Fasten off. Work border on other edge in same way.

appliqué bed cover
and pillows

This whimsical bedroom ensemble is a treat for the crocheter's imagination. Twelve large embellishments in four different patterns, and sixteen rosettes in four patterns are strewn over a duvet and pillowcases, then stitched in place to create a random effect of colorful blossoms blown over a snowy field. Mix and match patterns and colors by layering some of the small rosettes over the large motifs.

FINISHED MEASUREMENTS

- Large motifs 8½–10" (21.5–25.5 cm) across
- Small motifs 2½–4" (6.5–10 cm) across

MATERIALS

2 1 x 1¾ oz. (50 g) ball, approx. 137 yd. (115 m) long, of Rowan *Cotton Glace* (cotton) in #741 Poppy, #787 Hyacinth, #795 Butter, #802 Sunny, #809 Pier, #813 Zeal, #814 Shoot, #818 Hot Lips, and #819 In the Pink

- Size G-6 (4 mm) crochet hook, OR SIZE NECESSARY TO OBTAIN CORRECT GAUGE
- Dressmaker's pins
- Sewing thread to match
- Hand-sewing needle

NOTE Colors are meant to "mix and match"—use whatever combinations are most pleasing to you.

Bed cover and pillows

large motifs

Make 12 (3 of each pat from the foll colors): #741 Poppy, #819 In the Pink, #814 Shoot, #787 Hyacinth, and #809 Pier.

BUTTERFLY WINGS MOTIF

Ch 10, join with Sl st in first ch to form a ring.

Rnd 1 Ch 3, dc in ring, [3 ch, 2 dc in ring] 7 times, 3 ch, join with Sl st to 3rd st of 3 ch.

Rnd 2 Ch 3, dc in next dc, [5 ch, dc in next 2 dc] 7 times, 5ch, join.

Rnd 3 Ch 3, dc in next dc, ★ in next sp make [3 dc, 2 ch and 3 dc], dc in next 2 dc; rep from ★ around, join.

Rnd 4 Ch 3, dc in next 2 dc, ★ in next sp make [2 dc, 5 ch and 2 dc], miss 2 dc, dc in next 4 dc; rep from ★ around, join.

Rnd 5 Ch 3, dc in next 2 dc, ★ 3 ch, 6 tr in next sp, 3 ch, miss 2 dc, dc in next 4 dc; rep from ★ around, join.

Rnd 6 Ch 3, dc in next 2 dc, ★ 4 ch, [dc in next tr, 2 ch] 5 times, dc in next tr, 4 ch, dc in next 4 dc; rep from ★ around, join.

Rnd 7 Ch 3, dc in next 2 dc, ★ 5 ch, miss next sp, sc in next sp, [3 ch, sc in next sp] 4 times, 5 ch, miss next sp, dc in next 4 dc; rep from ★ around, join.

Rnd 8 Ch 3, dc in next 2 dc, ★ 6 ch, sc in next 3 ch

loop [3 ch, sc in next loop] 3 times, 6 ch, dc in next 4 dc; rep from ★ around, join.

Rnd 9 Ch 3, dc in next 2 dc, 2 dc in next sp, ★ 6 ch, sc in next loop, [3 ch, sc in next loop] twice, 6 ch, 2 dc in sp, dc in next 4 dc, 2 dc in next sp, rep from ★ around, join.

Rnd 10 Sl st in next 3 dc, 3 ch, dc in next dc, 2 dc in next sp, ★ 6 ch, sc in next loop, 3 ch, sc in next loop, 6 ch, 2 dc in next sp, dc in next 2 dc, 4 ch, miss 4 dc, dc in next 2 dc, 2 dc in next sp; rep from ★ around, join.

Rnd 11 Sl st in next 2 dc, 3 ch, dc in next dc, 2 dc in next sp, ★ 6 ch, sc in next loop, 6 ch, 2 dc in next sp, dc in next 2 dc, 6 ch, sc in next sp, 6 ch, miss 2 dc, dc in next 2 dc, 2 dc in next sp; rep from ★ around, join. Fasten off.

ENGLISH ROSE MOTIF

Ch 10, join with Sl st in first ch to form a ring.

Rnd 1 Ch 1, 18 sc in ring, join with Sl st to first sc.

Rnd 2 Ch 1, sc in same place as Sl st, ★ 5 ch, miss 2 sc, sc in next sc; rep from ★ 5 more times, 5 ch, join with Sl st to first sc.

Rnd 3 Ch 1, in each loop around make sc, hdc, 5 dc, hdc and sc (6 petals), join.

Rnd 4 Ch 1, sc in same place as Sl st, ★ 7 ch, insert hook in next loop from back to front of work, bring it out in next loop from front to back of work, yarn over, draw loop through, yarn over and draw through all loops on hook; rep from ★ around, join (6 loops).

Rnd 5 In each loop around make sc, hdc, dc, 7 tr, dc, hdc and sc (6 petals).

Rnd 6 Rep rnd 4.

Rnd 7 Sl st in first loop, 3 ch, 7 dc in same loop, 8 dc in each loop around (48 dc on round) join with Sl st to 3rd st of 3-ch.

Rnd 8 Ch 3, dc in next 2 dc, ★ 2 dc, dc in next 3 dc, 4 ch, sc in 4th ch from hook (picot made), dc in next 3 dc; rep from ★ around, join.

Rnd 9 Ch 3, dc in next 2 dc, ★ 2 ch, dc in next 3 dc, 1 ch, picot, 1 ch, dc in next 3 dc; rep from ★ around, join.

Rnd 10 Ch 3, dc in next 2 dc, ★ 2 ch, dc in next 3 dc; rep from ★ around, join.

Rnd 11 Ch 3, dc in next 2 dc, ★ 2 ch, dc in next 3 dc, 11 ch, dc in next 3 dc; rep from ★ around, join.

Rnd 12 Ch 3, dc in next 2 dc, ★ 2 ch, dc in next 3 dc, 11 dc in next sp, dc in next 3 dc; rep from ★ around, join. Fasten off.

MAGIC MOTIF

Ch 7, join with Sl st in first ch to form a ring.

Rnd 1 Ch 3, 15dc in ring. Join with Sl st to top of ch 3.

Rnd 2 Ch 7, ★ skip 1 dc, dc in next dc, ch 4; rep from ★ around, joining last ch 3 with Sl st to 3rd st of ch 7 (8 sps).

Rnd 3 Sl st in sp, ch 3, 7 dc in same sp, 8 dc in each following sp around, join with Sl st to top of ch 3. Work rnds 4–8 in back loops only.

Rnd 4 Ch 3, dc in next 7 dc, ★ ch 1, dc in next 8 dc. Rep from ★ around, ending with ch1, Sl st in top of ch 3.

Rnd 5 Ch 3, dc in next 7 dc, ★ ch 4, sc in 4th ch from hook (picot made), ch 1, skip 1 dc, dc in next 8 dc; rep from ★ around. Join.

style tip The bed cover and pillows will look their best if the motifs are randomly placed on the bed, so avoid placing them in any order. Do not arrange the flowers in rows or try to arrange the colors. To avoid color repeats, place the motifs in their random positions and then swap motifs where two colors appear together.

Rnd 6 Ch 3, dc in next 7 dc, ★ ch 1, a ch 4 p, ch 2, dc in next 8 dc; rep from ★ around. Join.

Rnd 7 Ch 3, dc in next 7 dc, ★ ch 8, dc in next 8 dc; rep from ★ around. Join.

Rnd 8 Ch 3, dc in next 7 dc, ★ 12 dc in sp, dc in next 8 dc; rep from ★ around. Join. Fasten off.

NOSEGAY MOTIF

Ch 8, join with Sl st in first ch to form a ring.

Rnd 1 Ch 3 (to count as 1 dc), 19 dc in ring. Join with Sl st to top of ch 3—20 sts.

Rnd 2 Ch 3, dc in same place as Sl st, 2 dc in each dc around; join with Sl st—40 sts.

Rnd 3 ★ Ch 7, skip 3 dc, sc in next dc; rep from ★ around, ending with ch 3, skip 3 dc, tr in same place as Sl st—10 loops.

Rnd 4 Ch 6, dc in top of tr, ★ ch 3, in center ch of next ch 7 loop make dc, ch 3 and dc; rep from ★ around, ending with ch 3, Sl st in 3rd ch of ch 6.

Rnd 5 Ch 3, ★ 4 dc in next ch-3 sp, dc in next dc, ch 3, dc in next dc; rep from ★ around, ending with ch 3, Sl st in 3rd ch of ch-3.

Rnd 6 Ch 3, dc in next 5 dc, ★ ch 3, sc in next sp, ch 3, dc in next 6 dc; rep from ★ around, ending with ch 3, Sl st in 3rd ch of ch-3.

Rnd 7 ★ Ch 7, skip 4 dc, sc in next dc, ch 7, dc in next dc; rep from ★ around, ending with ch 3, tr in same place as Sl st on previous round.

Rnd 8 Ch 3, 4 dc in top of tr, ★ ch 2, 5 dc in center of next loop; rep from ★ around, ending with hdc in 3rd ch of ch-3.

Rnd 9 Sc in sp, ch 1, dc between ch 3 and foll dc of next dc group, ★ ch 1, dc between 2nd and 3rd dc of same group, ch 1, dc between 3rd and 4th dc, ch 1, dc between 4th and 5th dc of same group, ch 1, sc in next sp (between groups), ch 1, dc between first and 2nd dc of next dc group; rep from ★ around, ending with ch 1, Sl st in first sc.

Rnd 10 Sc in same place as Sl st, ★ ch 5, skip 2 dc, in next sp make dc, ch 3 and dc, ch 5, skip 2 dc, sc in next sc; rep from ★ around, ending with ch 5, Sl st in first sc. Fasten off.

small motifs
Make 16 in total (4 of each pat) using all colors.

PRIMULA CIRCLE MOTIF
Ch 4, join with Sl st in first ch to form a ring.

Rnd 1 Ch 1, 11 sc into ring, join with a Sl st to first ch.

Rnd 2 Ch 1, 1 sc into same place, working into back loops only, work 2 sc into each st to end, join with a Sl st to first ch.

Rnd 3 Ch 3, ★ skip 1 sc, 1 sc into back loop of next sc, 2 ch, rep from ★ to end, join with a Sl st to first ch of 3-ch.

Rnd 4 Into each 2 ch sp work 1 sc, 1 dc, 2 tr, 1 dc and 1 sc, join with a Sl st to first sc. Fasten off.

SCALLOPED CIRCLE
Ch 6, join with Sl st in first ch to form a ring.

Rnd 1 Ch 3, 23 dc into ring, join with a Sl st to 3rd ch of 3-ch.

Rnd 2 Ch 5, 1 dc into Sl st, 1 ch, ★ skip 2 dc, [1 dc, 2 ch, 1 dc] into next dc, 1 ch, rep from ★ 6 times more, join with a Sl st to 3rd ch of ch-5.

Rnd 3 Sl st into 2 ch sp, 3 ch, [1 dc, 2 ch, 2 dc] into same sp, ★ 1 sc into 1 ch sp, [2 dc, 2 ch, 2 dc]

into 2 ch sp, rep from ★ 6 times more, 1 sc into 1 ch sp, join with a Sl st into 3rd ch of 3-ch.

Rnd 4 Sl st into 2 ch sp, 3 ch [2 dc, 1 ch, 3 dc] into same sp, ★ 1 sc before next sc, 1 sc after the same sc, [3 dc, 1 ch, 3 dc] into 2 ch sp, rep from ★ 6 times more, 1 sc before next sc, 1 sc after the same sc, join with a Sl st to 3rd ch of ch-3. Fasten off.

SMALL ROSETTE
Ch 8, join with Sl st in first ch to form a ring.

Rnd 1 3 ch, 2 dc in ring, [5 ch, sc in 3rd ch from hook, 2 ch, 3 dc, 3 dc in ring] 6 times, 5 ch, sc in 3rd ch from hook, 2 ch, Sl st into 3rd ch of ch-3.

Rnd 2 Sc in next dc, [10 ch, sc in center dc of next group] 6 times, 10 ch, Sl st in first sc. Fasten off.

ROSETTE
Ch 9, join with Sl st in first ch to form a ring.

Rnd 1 Ch 3, 2 dc in ring, ★ 6 ch, Sl st sideways in last dc made, 3 dc in ring; rep from ★ 4 times, 6 ch, Sl st in last dc, Sl st in 3rd ch of ch-3.

Rnd 2 Sl st in center dc of any 3-dc group ★ work 11 dc sts into 6-ch loop, Sl st in center dc of next 3-dc group; rep from ★ 5 more times, Sl st in first stitch. Fasten off.

finishing
Arrange the motifs on bedspread and pillowcases, centering some of the small motifs on top of the larger ones. Scatter the rest of the small motifs in between the larger ones. Pin in position, and hand-stitch in place with matching thread.

tweedy bath **mat**

A washable bouclé yarn makes this bath mat both practical and soft to the touch. The tweedy look works as well in a contemporary setting as it does with the clawfoot tub shown here. Pick three shades to coordinate with your towels. The broken check pattern works up fast and easy on a large hook.

FINISHED MEASUREMENTS
- Width 22" (56 cm)
- Length 29" (73.5 cm)

MATERIALS

5 1 x 6 oz. (170 g) skein, approx. 185 yd. (167 cm) long, of Lion Brand *Homespun* (acrylic/polyester) in #309 Deco (A), #389 Spring Green (B), and #391 Blue Sky (C)
- Size K-10½ (6.5 mm) crochet hook, OR SIZE NECESSARY TO OBTAIN CORRECT GAUGE

GAUGE
10 dc = 4" (10 cm)

6 rows in pattern = 5" (12.5 cm). BE SURE TO CHECK THE GAUGE.

BODY PATTERN
Row 1 With appropriate color, hdc in first st; [dc into skipped st 2 rows below, ch 1, skip 1 st] across, hdc into last st.

Bath mat

With A, ch 50. Sc in 2nd ch from hook and in each ch across—49 sts. Ch 2, turn at end of this and all rows.

Row 1 With A, hdc in first st, [ch 1, skip 1 st, dc in next st] across, ending last rep with hdc. Drop A; attach B.

Row 2 With B, rep row 1 of body pattern. Drop B, attach C.

Row 3 With C, rep row 1 of body pattern. Drop C, pick up A.

Rep rows 1–3 until piece measures 27" (68.5 cm) from beg, ending with C.

Next row With A, [hdc in next st, dc into skipped st 2 rows below] across, ending with hdc in last st. Ch 1, turn.

border
Row 1 With A, ★ sc in each st across end, work 3 sc in corner; working down side, sc evenly to corner, 3 sc in corner; rep from ★; Sl st in first sc to join. Do not turn.

Row 2 Working in back loops only, ch 3, (counts as dc); dc in each sc around, working 5 dc in center sc of 3-sc corner. Fasten off A. Turn.

Row 3 With WS facing, attach B in front loop of any st, Sl st in front loop only of each st around, taking care not to pull work too tightly. Fasten off.

autumn leaves afghan

As soon as the air gets nippy, you'll want to reach for this small, chunky afghan made of hexagons worked in two different color combinations. Here, the inner ring is worked in camel, brown, and pumpkin, while the center hexagon and outer ring are crocheted in berry, brown, and rust. The hexagons give an interesting shape to a piece that will warm up any room in a flash. A simple border completes the throw.

FINISHED MEASUREMENTS

- Approx. 52" (132 cm) across

MATERIALS

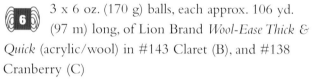

3 x 6 oz. (170 g) balls, each approx. 106 yd. (97 m) long, of Lion Brand *Wool-Ease Thick & Quick* (acrylic/wool) in #143 Claret (B), and #138 Cranberry (C)

- 2 x 6 oz. (170 g) balls, each approx. 106 yd. (97 m) long, of Lion Brand *Wool-Ease Thick & Quick* (acrylic/wool) in #135 Spice (A), and #187 Goldenrod (E)
- 1 x 6 oz. (170 g) ball, approx. 106 yd. (97 m) long, of Lion Brand *Wool-Ease Thick & Quick* (acrylic/wool) in #133 Pumpkin (D)
- Size M/N-13 (9 mm) crochet hook, OR SIZE NECESSARY TO OBTAIN CORRECT GAUGE

GAUGE

Motif = 10" (25.5 cm) across. BE SURE TO CHECK THE GAUGE.

STITCH GLOSSARY

Dec sc Pull up a loop in next 2 sts, yo and through 3 loops on hook.

Dec hdc Yo, pull up a loop in next st, yo and through 2 loops; skip next st, yo, pull up a loop in next st, yo and through 2 loops; yo and through 3 loops on hook.

Afghan

NOTE Motifs are made in 2 different color combinations, as foll:

Motif 1: make 13 using A, B, and C.

Motif 2: make 6 using D, B, and E.

With appropriate color, ch 5; Sl st in first ch to form a ring.

Rnd 1 (RS) Ch 4, 2 tr in ring; [ch 1, 3 tr in ring] 5 times; ch 1, join with Sl st in top of ch 4. Ch 1, turn.

Rnd 2 (WS) Sc in ch-1 sp, [ch 5, skip 3 tr, sc in next ch-1 sp] 6 times, ending last rep with Sl st in first sc. Fasten off color. Turn.

Rnd 3 (RS) Join 2nd color in any ch-5 sp; [hdc, 2 dc, 3 tr, 2 dc, hdc] group in each ch-5 sp around. Fasten off 2nd color. Do not turn.

Rnd 4 (RS) Join 3rd color in top of first hdc of group, ch 4 (counts as tr) ★★, [dc in 2 dc, hdc in 3 tr, dc in 2 dc, tr in hdc, ch 1 for corner, ★ tr in next hdc] rep from ★★ around, ending last rep at ★; Sl st in top of ch-4 to join. Fasten off.

finishing

Join motifs, with motif 1 in center, and 6 x motif 2 on each side. Join rem 12 x motif 1 in each side around. Motifs may be joined with whipstitch through matching back loops, or Sl st tog through matching back loops.

border

Rnd 1 Join E in any ch-1 corner, working in back loops only, sc in each st around, working dec sc on inside corners where motifs meet, and [sc, ch 1, sc] on each of the outside corners—approx. 9 sc on each side. Sl st in first sc to join. Do not turn.

Rnd 2 Ch 4 (counts as hdc, ch 1), ★ [skip 1 st, hdc in next st, ch 1] 4 times along side, skip 1 st, [hdc, ch 2, hdc] for outside corners, or dec hdc for inside corners. Rep from ★ around. Join in 3rd ch of ch-4. Fasten off.

colorful pillow trims

These fanciful trims are easy and fun to make. Choose a medium weight cotton yarn so they work up fast. Buy throw pillows in cotton prints, or stitch up reversible pillow covers with different prints front and back. Yarn colors can contrast or blend with the pillow fabrics as inspiration dictates.

FINISHED MEASUREMENTS

Each trim is for a 16" (40.5 cm) square pillow

MATERIALS

4 1 x 1¾ oz. (50 g) skein, approx. 108 yd. (99 m) long, of Tahki Stacy Charles *Cotton Classic* (cotton) in #3559 Gold, #3200 Ivory, #3469 Rose, #3936 Lavender, and #3715 Green
- Size G-6 (4 mm) crochet hook, OR SIZE NECESSARY TO OBTAIN CORRECT GAUGE
- Hand-sewing needle
- Sewing thread to match
- 2 x 18" (46 cm) squares of fabric per pillow (minimum)
- 16" (40.5 cm) pillow form per pillow

GAUGE

4 sc = 1" (2.5 cm). BE SURE TO CHECK THE GAUGE.

STITCH GLOSSARY

Picot Ch 3; Sl st into first ch.
Tr group Holding all rem loops on hook, [yo 2 times, pull up loop, yo and through 2 loops twice] 3 times; yo and through 4 loops to close group.

Gold trim

Row 1 Ch 272; sc in 2nd ch from hook and in each ch across—271 sc. Ch 1, turn.
Row 2 Sc in each sc across. Ch 1, turn.
Row 3 Sc in sc; ★ ch 5, skip 4 sc, sc in next sc, ch 5, skip 4 sc, [dc, ch 3, dc] in next sc; rep from ★ across. Ch 1, turn.
Row 4 ★ [Hdc, picot] 3 times in ch-3 sp; hdc in same sp; 5 sc in ch-5 sp; Sl st in sc, 5 sc in ch-5 sp; rep from ★ across. Fasten off.

Ivory trim

Row 1 Ch 272; sc in 2nd ch from hook and in each ch across—271 sc. Ch 1, turn.
Row 2 Sc in each sc across. Ch 1, turn.
Row 3 Ch 7; ★ skip 3 sts, [tr, ch 4, tr group] in next sc; rep from ★ across. Fasten off.

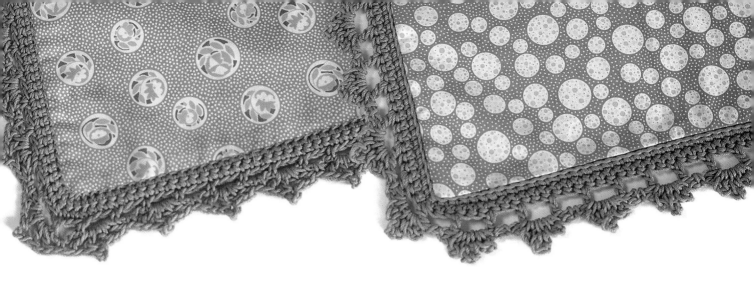

Rose trim

Row 1 Ch 272; sc in 2nd ch from hook and in each ch across—271 sc. Ch 1, turn.
Row 2 Sc in each sc across. Ch 1, turn.
Row 3 Sc in sc; [ch 3, skip 2 sts, sc in next st] across. Ch 1, turn.
Row 4 Sl st in ch 3, ch 4 (counts as dc, ch 1), dc in same sp; picot; [dc, ch 1, dc] in same ch-3 sp; ★ sc in next ch-3 sp; [dc, ch 1, dc, picot, dc, ch 1, dc] in next ch-3 sp; rep from ★ across. Fasten off.

Lavender trim

Row 1 Ch 272; sc in 2nd ch from hook and in each ch across—271 sc. Ch 1, turn.
Row 2 Sc in each sc across. Ch 5, turn.
Row 3 [Skip 2 sts, dc in next st, ch 2] across; dc in last sc. Ch 1, turn.
Row 4 ★ [Sc, ch 3, sc, ch 5, sc, ch 3, sc] in ch-2 sp; ch 1, skip dc, Sl st in ch-2 sp, ch 1, skip dc; rep from ★ across, ending last rep with sc in last st. Fasten off.

Green trim

Row 1 Ch 272; sc in 2nd ch from hook and in each ch across—271 sc. Ch 1, turn.
Row 2 Sc in each sc across. Ch 1, turn.
Row 3 Sc in first sc; [ch 3, 3 dc in base of ch-3, skip 2 sts, Sl st in next st] across, ending last rep with dc in last st.

finishing

Cut fabric for case at least ½" (1.5 cm) larger on all sides than pillow form. With RS tog, sew case with ½" (1.5 cm) seams, leaving opening for form. Turn RS out. Fold trim in half, then half again to mark the 4 quarters. Matching sections of trim to sides of pillow, sew in place with small stitches. Insert form, then stitch opening closed.

floral trim bag

The rich shades of multitone yarn add depth and dimension to a handbag that's soft, striking, and bursting with charm. Bag, handles, flowers, and leaves are all crocheted separately, then the bag and handles are felted before the flowers are stitched on.

FINISHED MEASUREMENTS
- Width 12" (30.5 cm) after felting
- Height 11" (28 cm) after felting, excluding handles

MATERIALS
 2 x 3½ oz. (100 g) skeins, each approx. 220 yd. (200 m) long, of Cascade Yarns *Cascade 220 Quatro* (wool) in #9433 Cherry Mix (MC)
- 1 x 3½ oz. (100 g) skein, approx. 220 yd. (200 m) long, of Cascade Yarns *Cascade 220* (wool) in #9444 Orange (A), #2411 Burgundy (B), and #8903 Green (C)
- Size H-8 (5 mm) crochet hook, OR SIZE NECESSARY TO OBTAIN CORRECT GAUGE
- Stitch marker

GAUGE
15 dc and 7 rows = 4" (10 cm). BE SURE TO CHECK THE GAUGE.

> **fashion tip** Make extra flowers to trim the ends of a scarf crocheted in the main color to match the bag.

Bag

base
With MC, ch 34 very loosely (this is important for felting to work correctly).
Rnd 1 Dc in 4th ch from hook (counts as 2 dc), dc in each of next 28 ch, 5 dc in last ch, working into rem loops on opposite side of ch, work dc in each of next 28 ch, 4 dc in last ch; join with Sl st to top of ch 3.
Rnd 2 Ch 3 (counts as dc), dc in each of next 30 dc, 3 dc in each of next 3 dc, dc in each of next 31 dc, 3 dc in each of last 3 dc; join with Sl st to top of ch 3.
Rnd 3 Ch 3 (counts as dc), dc in each of next 32 dc, 3 dc in each of next 5 dc, dc in each of next 33 dc, 3 dc in each of next 5 dc, dc in each of last 2 dc; join with Sl st to top of ch 3. Place a marker at end of last rnd.

body of bag
Rnd 1 Ch 1, sc in same sp, sc in back loop of each dc around; join with Sl st to first sc—98 sc.
Rnd 2 Ch 3 (counts as dc), dc in each st around; join with Sl st to top of ch 3.
Rep rnd 2 until body of bag measures 10½" (26.5 cm) from marked rnd. Fasten off.

straps (make 2)
With MC, ch 9 loosely. Join with Sl st to first ch to form a ring.
Rnd 1 Ch 3 (counts as dc), dc in next ch and each ch around; join with Sl st to top of ch 3—9 dc.

Rnd 2 Ch 3 (counts as dc), dc in each dc around; join with Sl st to top of ch 3.
Rep rnd 2 until strap measures 21" (53.5 cm). Fasten off.

finishing

To secure top edge before felting, thread a length of MC through final rnd and ease in top edge slightly.

FELTING

Weave in all yarn ends. Set your washing machine at lowest water level (enough to just cover pieces), hottest temperature, and highest agitation. Add body of bag, straps and an old towel (for added abrasion). Using a small amount of liquid detergent, begin washing and check on pieces approx. every 5 minutes until desired felting of fabric is achieved; the stitch definition should be almost unrecognizable. Remove pieces and rinse by hand in lukewarm water. Roll pieces in towels to remove excess water. Dry flat.

flower

Make 5 with A as Color 1 and B as Color 2.
Make 5 with B as Color 1 and A as Color 2.
With Color 1, ch 4; join with Sl st to first ch to form a ring.
Rnd 1 Ch 1, 10 sc in ring; join with Sl st to first sc.
Rnd 2 Ch 1, sc in same sp, ★ ch 3, miss next sc,

sc in next sc; rep from ★ 3 times more, ch 3; join with Sl st to first sc. Break Color 1.
Rnd 3 Working behind rnd 2, join MC with Sl st to any missed sc from rnd 2, ch 1, sc in same sp, ★ ch 4, sc in next missed sc; rep from ★ 3 times more, ch 4; join with Sl st to first sc.
Rnd 4 Sl st in first ch-4 sp, ch 1, (sc, 3 hdc, sc) all in same sp, ★ (sc, 3 hdc, sc) all in next ch-4 sp; rep from ★ 3 times more; join with Sl st to first sc. Break MC.
Rnd 5 Join Color 2 with Sl st to any center hdc of 3 hdc group, ch 1, sc in same sp, ★ ch 3, sc in sp between next 2 sc, ch 3, sc in center hdc of next 3 hdc group; rep from ★ 3 times more, ch 3, sc in sp between next 2 sc, ch 3; join with Sl st to first sc. Fasten off.

leaf (make 14)

With C ch 8.
Row 1 Sc in 2nd ch from hook, sc in next ch, hdc in next ch, dc in next ch, hdc in next ch, sc in next ch, 3 sc in last ch; working along opposite side of foundation ch, work sc in next ch, hdc in next ch, dc in next ch, hdc in next ch, sc in next ch, 2 sc in last ch; join with Sl st to first sc. Fasten off. Sew flowers and leaves in position as shown along top edge of bag. Sew ends of handles in position to WS.

table **centerpiece**

Rings, wheels, and flower motifs in pastel shades are combined to make this cool modern design that will add a soft touch to any tabletop or sideboard. This is a perfect project to make on the go as the motifs are crocheted individually and joined together at the end.

FINISHED MEASUREMENTS
- Length approx. 11½" (29 cm) at longest point
- Width approx. 8¾" (22 cm) at widest point

MATERIALS
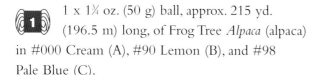 1 x 1¾ oz. (50 g) ball, approx. 215 yd. (196.5 m) long, of Frog Tree *Alpaca* (alpaca) in #000 Cream (A), #90 Lemon (B), and #98 Pale Blue (C).
- Size B-1/C-2 (2.5 mm) crochet hook OR SIZE NECESSARY TO OBTAIN CORRECT GAUGE
- Tapestry needle

YOU MAY ALSO NEED
- Size S (19 mm), P-15 (10 mm), J-10 (6 mm) crochet hooks

GAUGE
Flower motif = 2" (5 cm). BE SURE TO CHECK THE GAUGE.

Centerpiece

flower
Make 3 using A to start and B for rnd 2.
Ch 6, join with Sl st to first ch to form a ring.
Rnd 1 Ch 3, 18 dc into ring, join with Sl st to top of 3 ch.
Rnd 2 Ch 1, 1 sc in first dc, 5 ch, skip 1, ★ 1 sc, 5 ch, skip 1, rep from ★ all round, join with Sl st to first ch; fasten off.
Rnd 3 Join B at first ch of previous rnd, ch 1 [1 sc, 5 dc, 1 sc] into each 5-ch sp, join with Sl st to first ch; fasten off.

wheel
Make 8 using C.
Rnd 1 Make a yarn loop (see page 99), work 12 sc into loop and pull tight to make closed ring; join with Sl st to first sc.
Rnd 2 Ch 7 (counts as first tr and ch sp). ★ Skip 1, 1 tr, ch 3; rep from ★ all round, join with Sl st to 3rd ch of first ch.
Rnd 3 Ch 2 (count as first hdc), 7 hdc into first 3-ch sp, ★ 8 hdc into next 3-ch sp, rep from ★ 4 times more, join with Sl st to first ch; fasten off.

large circle
Make 17 using B.
Wrap yarn around two fingers—or size S (19 mm)

crochet hook—28 times. Work sc into ring made until all wrapped yarn is covered with sc, join with Sl st to first sc; Fasten off.

medium circle

Make 38, using all 3 colors.
Wrap yarn around one finger—or size P-15 (10 mm) crochet hook—28 times. Work sc into ring made until all wrapped yarn is covered with sc, join with Sl st to first sc; fasten off.

small circle

Make 20 using yarns A and C.
Wrap yarn around a size J-10 (6 mm) crochet hook 28 times. Work sc into ring made until all wrapped yarn is covered with sc, join with Sl st to first sc; fasten off.

finishing

Lay out the motifs on a flat surface, and using the photo as a guide, combine until you have a pleasing arrangement. Make extra small or medium motifs to fill any gaps, as necessary. Thread a tapestry needle with a length of the palest colored yarn used in the two motfs you are joining, and secure on the back of motif at the top left of your arrangement. Stitch this motif to the adjacent one, taking care to keep your stitches concealed beneath the crocheted work. Continue stitching the motifs together, working roughly in rows, until the centerpiece is finished. Fasten off.

style tip Make a long table runner by using more motifs. Use fewer for a smaller centerpiece—you could add motif designs of your own to personalize the design.

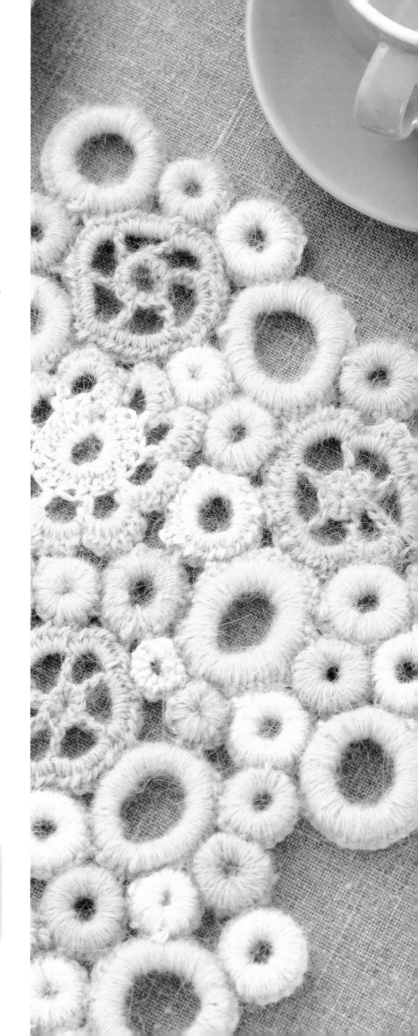

album cover

Store your scrap-booking pages and family snapshots in style with this tactile album cover. This project makes an ideal gift—collect pictures of you and your best friend, then present them to her in this beautiful album on her birthday. The design can be easily altered to fit an album you have previously filled with pictures.

FINISHED MEASUREMENTS

- Length approx. 21" (53 cm)
- Width approx. 8" (20 cm)

NOTE The cover fits an album 9 x 7¾" (23 x 20 cm) and 2" (5 cm) thick.

MATERIALS

 1 x 3½ oz. (100 g) ball, approx. 150 yd. (137 m) long, of Blue Sky Alpacas *Blue Sky Cotton* (cotton) in #617 Lotus (A), #618 Orchid (B), #608 Lemonade (C), and #602 Honeydew (D).
- Size G-6 (4 mm) crochet hook OR SIZE NECESSARY TO OBTAIN CORRECT GAUGE
- Tapestry needle

GAUGE

16 dc and 9 rows = 4" (10 cm). BE SURE TO CHECK THE GAUGE.

Cover

With A, ch 36.
Row 1 (RS) 1 dc into 4th ch from hook, then 1 dc into each following ch—34 sts; turn.
Row 2 Ch 3 (counts as first dc), 33 dc; turn.
Row 3 Rep row 2.
Row 4 Ch 4 (counts as first dc and 1 ch sp), skip 1, 1 dc, ★ ch 1, skip 1, 1 dc, rep from ★ to end; fasten off, turn.
Row 5 Join B; rep row 2.
Rep last row 15 times more—20 rows; fasten off, turn.
Row 21 Join C; ch 1 (counts as first sc), 33 sc; fasten off, turn.
Row 22 Join B, then work as row 21; fasten off, turn.
Row 23 Join D, then work as row 21; fasten off, turn.
Row 24 Join B, then work as row 21; fasten off, turn.
Row 25 Join A, then work as row 21; fasten off, turn.
Row 26 Join B, then work as row 21; fasten off, turn.
Row 27 Join C; ch 2 (counts as first hdc), 33 hdc; fasten off, turn.
Row 28 Join D, then work as row 27; fasten off, turn.
Row 29 and 30 Rep last two rows.
Row 31 Join A, then work as row 27; fasten off, turn.
Rows 32–35 Rep rows 27–30.
Row 36 Rep row 27.
Row 37 Rep row 31.
Rows 38–41 Rep 27–30.
Row 42 Join B, then work as row 21; fasten off, turn.

Row 43 Join A, then work as row 21; fasten off, turn.

Row 44 Join B, then work as row 21; fasten off, turn.

Row 45 Join D, then work as row 21; fasten off, turn.

Row 46 Join B, then work as row 21; fasten off, turn.

Row 47 Join C, then work as row 21; fasten off, turn.

Row 48 Join B, then work as row 2; fasten off, turn.

Rep last row 15 times—63 rows; fasten off, turn.

Row 64 Join A, then work as row 4; turn.

Row 65 Rep row 2.

Rep last row twice; fasten off.

embellishments

MOTIF 1

With C, ch 4, join with Sl st to first ch to form a ring.

Rnd 1 Work 8 sc into ring, join with Sl st to first sc; fasten off.

Rnd 2 Join D, 2 sc into each sc—16 sts; fasten off. Work 1 rnd of surface chain: using A, draw a loop of yarn through to the right side at any point between rnd 1 and 2, keeping the working yarn to the back of the motif. Work Sl st all round the motif, covering the join between rnds 1 and 2 by inserting the hook through the work and picking up the thread below.

Make one more motif using D for rnd 1 and C for rnd 2.

MOTIF 2

Using C, ch 4, join with Sl st to first ch to form a ring.

Rnd 1 Work 8 sc into ring, join with Sl st to first sc.

Rnd 2 Work 2 sc into each sc, join with Sl st to first sc—16 sts.

Rnd 3 Work 2 sc into each sc, join with Sl st to first sc—32 sts; fasten off.

MOTIF 3

Using A, ch 4, join with Sl st to first ch to form a ring.

Rnd 1 Work 8 sc into ring, join with Sl st to first sc.

Rnd 2 Work 2 sc into each sc, join with Sl st to first sc—16 sts; fasten off.

Make one more motif using C.

MOTIF 4

Using D, ch 3, join with Sl st to first ch to form a ring.

Rnd 1 6 dc into ring, join with Sl st to first dc; fasten off.

Make 4 more using D. Make 3 using C, and 3 using A.

finishing

Thread a tapestry needle with a length of B. Turn under one end of the finished cover so that the area worked in A is turned to the WS. Stitch along the short sides of the turning to form a pocket. Rep at the other end of the finished cover; the album fits into these pockets when the cover is in place.

Make a chain to hold the album cover in place. On the inside of the front cover, join A to the A stripe near the album spine at the top of the book, then join at the other end of the stripe at the bottom of the album cover. Rep for inside of back cover.

Thread a tapestry needle with a short length of D and secure to the WS of one motif 4 of the same color, at the center. Pass the needle, from the RS to the WS, through the center of one motif 3 in A and through the center of the motif 2. Draw the three motifs together and secure the thread on the WS of motif 2. Leave the thread on the needle and then use this to stitch the joined motifs onto the striped area of the cover. Rep to join one motif 4 in D to the remaining motif 3, and stitch in place at the corner of the cover. Stitch two motif 1s next to this, using the appropriate colored thread. Using the photo as a guide, stitch the remaining motifs in place, using the appropriate colored thread.

floral tiebacks

These cute tiebacks will add a splash of color to any window. The flower motifs are built up in layers of petals to create a bright, three-dimensional bouquet. The flowers are accented with pretty embroidery stitches, while leaves and a sturdy crocheted band complete the design. Simple crochet loops make for easy hanging.

FINISHED MEASUREMENTS

- Length 24" (60 cm)

MATERIALS

4 1 x 3½ oz. (100 g) ball, approx. 230 yd. (210 m) long, of Patons *100% Cotton* (cotton) in #02718 Azalea (A), #02707 Pansy (B), #02706 Foxglove (C), and #02705 Peacock (D)
- 1 skein orange stranded embroidery cotton
- Size E-4 (3.5 mm) crochet hook OR SIZE NECESSARY TO OBTAIN CORRECT GAUGE
- Embroidery needle
- Tapestry needle

GAUGE

20 dc and 24 rows = 4" (10 cm). BE SURE TO CHECK THE GAUGE.

Tiebacks

band (make 2)

With B, ch 121.
Row 1 Sc in 3rd ch from hook and in each ch across; turn.
Row 2 Ch 2 (counts as 1 sc), sc in each sc of previous row—120 sts.
Rep last row 6 more times—8 rows; fasten off.

HANGING LOOP

Rejoin yarn at one corner of band. Work 2 Sl st along narrow edge of band (each st is the depth of a row), ch 6, skip 4 rows, 2 Sl st over rem 2 rows; fasten off.
Rep at other end of band then rep twice on the 2nd band.

leaf (make 8)

With D, ch 10.
Row 1 Sc in 2nd ch from hook, 1 hdc, 1 dc, 2 tr, 1 dc, 1 hdc, 1 sc, 1 Sl st, ch 1; turn.
Row 2 Work along the other side of foundation ch; 1 Sl st, 1 sc, 1 hdc, 1 dc, 2 tr, 1 dc, 1 hdc, 2 sc; fasten off.

dahlia (make 4)

With D, ch 3.
Rnd 1 (RS) 6 sc in first ch of foundation ch, Sl st to 3rd ch of foundation ch—7 sts (first 2 ch of foundation ch counts as 1 sc).

Rnd 2 (RS) Ch 3, ★ sc in next sc, ch 1, rep from ★ 6 times, Sl st to 2nd ch of 3 ch at beg of rnd—7 ch-sps; fasten off.

Rnd 3 (RS) Join A in any ch sp; [1 Sl st, ch 2, 2 dc, ch 2, 1 Sl st] into each ch sp—7 petals; turn.

Rnd 4 (WS) Working behind this last rnd of petals and into each of the sc of the 2nd rnd: ch 4 (counts as 1 sc and 2 ch), ★ 1 sc into next sc, ch 2, rep from ★ 5 times more, Sl st to 2nd ch of 4 ch at beg of rnd—7 ch sp; turn.

Rnd 5 (RS) [1 Sl st, ch 3, 2 tr, ch 3, 1 Sl st] into each ch sp—7 petals; turn.

Rnd 6 (WS) Working behind this last rnd of petals and into each of the sc of 4th rnd: ch 5 (counts as 1 sc and 3 ch), ★ 1 sc into next sc, ch 3, rep from ★ 5 times more, Sl st to 2nd ch of 5 ch at beg of rnd—7 ch sp; turn.

Rnd 7 (RS) Join C at beg of any ch sp; [1 Sl st, ch 3, 3 tr, ch 3, 1 Sl st] into each ch sp—7 petals; turn.

Rnd 8 (WS) Working behind this last rnd of petals and into each of the sc of the 6th rnd: ch 6 (counts as 1 sc and 4 ch), ★ 1 sc into next sc, ch 4, rep from ★ 5 times more, Sl st to 2nd ch of 6 ch at beg of rnd—7 ch sp; turn.

Rnd 9 (RS) [1 Sl st, ch 3, 2 tr, ch 3, 1 Sl st, ch 3, 2 tr, ch 3, 1 Sl st] in each ch sp—14 petals; fasten off.

daisy (make 2)

With col D, ch 3.

Rnd 1 Work 7 sc in first ch of foundation ch, Sl st to 3rd ch of foundation ch—8 sts (first 2 ch of foundation ch counts as 1 sc).

Rnd 2 Ch 2, 1 sc in base of 2 ch, 2 sc into each sc of previous rnd working into back loop only of each st, Sl st to 2nd ch of 2 ch—16 sc (2 ch counts as 1 sc).

Rnd 3 Join B with a Sl st to any sc of 2nd rnd, working into back loop only, ch 9, Sl st back into same st, ★ Sl st into next st, working into back loop

only, ch 9, Sl st back into same st, rep from ★ into each sc of 2nd rnd—16 ch loops.

Rnd 4 Sl st into front loop of sc from 2nd rnd where joined in col B, ch 7, Sl st back into same st, ★ Sl st, into next sc from 2nd rnd, working into front loop only, ch 7, Sl st back into same st, rep from ★ into front loop of each sc of 2nd rnd—16 ch loops; fasten off.

michaelmas daisy (make 4)

With D, ch 3.

Rnd 1 Work 7 sc in first ch of foundation ch, Sl st to 3rd ch of foundation ch—8 sts (first 2 ch of foundation ch counts as 1 sc); fasten off.

Rnd 2 Join B with a Sl st to any sc of first rnd, working into back loop only, ch 8, Sl st back into same st, ★ Sl st, into next st, working into back loop only, ch 8, Sl st back into same st, rep from ★ into each sc of first rnd—8 ch loops.

Rnd 3 Sl st into front loop of sc from first rnd where joined in col B, ch 6, Sl st back into same st, ★ Sl st, into next sc from first rnd, working into front loop only, ch 6, Sl st back into same st, rep from ★ into front loop of each sc of first rnd—8 ch loops; fasten off.

chrysanthemum (make 2)

With D, ch 3.

Rnd 1 Work 5 sc in first ch of foundation ch, Sl st to 3rd ch of foundation ch—6 sts (first 2 ch of foundation ch counts as 1 sc).

Rnd 2 Ch 2, 1 sc in base of 2 ch, 2 sc into each sc of prev rnd working into back loop only of each st, Sl st to 2nd ch of 2 ch—12 sc (2 ch counts as 1 sc); fasten off.

Rnd 3 Join A with a Sl st to any sc of 2nd rnd, working into back loop only; ★ ch 8, 1 sc into 3rd ch from hook, 1 sc into each of rem 5 ch, Sl st in back loop of next sc on 2nd rnd, rep from ★ all round, working last Sl st into front loop of sc on

2nd rnd where joined in B—12 petals.

Rnd 4 Working into front loops only of sc on 2nd rnd; ★ ch 7, 1 sc in 3rd ch from hook, 1 sc into each of rem 4 ch, Sl st in front loop of next sc of 2nd rnd, rep from ★ all round, working last Sl st into first Sl st of rnd—12 inner petals; fasten off.

Rnd 5 Join C with a Sl st into front loop only of any st on first rnd; ★ ch 6, Sl st back into same st, ch 6, Sl st to next st, rep from ★ all round—12 ch loops; fasten off.

embroidery

Weave in all yarn ends and secure; trim off any excess yarn. Thread an embroidery needle with some of the stranded cotton and, using the photo opposite as a guide, work a circle of chain sts around the center of each dahlia. Work chain st in the center loops of each chrysanthemum. On the Michelmas daisy, make 6 long sts around the center of the flower, radiating out from the center point. Work a large French knot at the center of each of the daisies. Lightly steam each of the flowers and arrange the petals. Do not press. Leave to dry.

finishing

Take each band and thread a tapestry needle with yarn in a contrasting color. Use this to mark the point 30 sts in from one end and 4 rows up from the long edge on each band. This marks the center of the floral-motif position. Fold one band in half widthwise and lay out, with the fold to the left. Arrange half of the flowers and leaves around the point marked with the thread, using the photo on page 75 as a guide. Sew in place using a tapestry needle and appropriate color yarn. This completes the right tieback. Rep with the remaining band but lay out with the fold to the right. Reverse the positioning of the remaining flowers and leaves, so a mirror image is created on the left tieback.

pearly napkin rings

These napkin rings are well worth the effort of working with an unfamiliar material.

The pretty pearls and subtle tones make for an elegant table decoration, while the

unique technique produces a wonderfully fresh and contemporary modern-classic.

To complete the look, check for flammable materials, then make a slightly larger

version to sit around a glass jar, and place a small votive candle inside.

FINISHED MEASUREMENTS
- Height approx. 1½" (4 cm)
- Diameter approx. 2" (5 cm)

MATERIALS
- 9 yd. (8.25 m) flexible copper-colored wire (per ring)
- Size E-4 (3.5 mm) crochet hook
- 40 pearls in assorted sizes (per ring)
- Wire-cutters
- Snipe-nose pliers

GAUGE
NOTE The nature of working with wire for the first time may give your napkin rings a different gauge each time. Try to keep the stitch sizes the same, and remember: small inconsistencies will add to the charm of the rings.

Napkin ring

Thread all of the beads onto the wire.
Ch 25; Sl st into first ch to form a ring.
Rnd 1 Ch 3, dc into each ch around, incorporating the pearls by sliding them down the wire and forming 1 dc behind the bead. Space the beads irregularly to create a random look. Join with Sl st into the top of the first dc.
Rnd 2 and 3 Rep rnd 1.

finishing
To complete the ring, clip the end of the wire and weave in the loose ends—use the pliers to neaten them so that there are no sharp ends.

dresser-top **pots**

These funky crochet pots will add a touch of sparkle to your dressing table. Use them to organize your makeup brushes, cotton wool, and pieces of jewelry. Modern ribbon yarn and sparkling lamè will bring a glamourous touch to your boudoir—the designs have sparkling trims or tassels to add a luxurious element to the finished designs.

FINISHED MEASUREMENTS

SMALL POT

- Diameter approx. 2¾" (7 cm)
- Height approx. 2⅝" (6.5 cm)
- Lid approx. ¾" (2 cm) deep, excluding trim

LARGE POT

- Diameter approx. 6" (15 cm)
- Height approx. 3" (7.5 cm)
- Lid approx. ¾" (2 cm) deep

MATERIALS

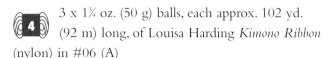 3 x 1¾ oz. (50 g) balls, each approx. 102 yd. (92 m) long, of Louisa Harding *Kimono Ribbon* (nylon) in #06 (A)

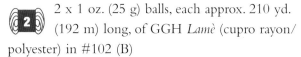 2 x 1 oz. (25 g) balls, each approx. 210 yd. (192 m) long, of GGH *Lamè* (cupro rayon/ polyester) in #102 (B)

- Size G-6 (4 mm) crochet hook, OR SIZE NECESSARY TO OBTAIN CORRECT GAUGE

GAUGE

Small pot base = 2¾" (7 cm). BE SURE TO CHECK THE GAUGE.

Small pot

NOTE Work with 1 strand each of A and B held together.

Rnd 1 Make a yarn loop (see page 99), then work 8 sc into loop, pull tight to make closed ring, join with Sl st into first sc.

Rnd 2 Ch 1, work 2 sc in each sc, join with Sl st to first chain—16 sts.

Rnd 3 Ch 1, 1 sc in first sc, 2 sc in next sc, ★ 1 sc in next sc, 2 sc in next sc, rep from ★ around; join with Sl st to first ch—24 sts.

Rnd 4 Ch 1, 1 sc in first sc, 2 sc in next sc, ★ 1 sc in next sc, 2 sc in next sc, rep from ★ all round, join with Sl st to first ch—36 sts.

Rnd 5 Ch 1, work evenly in sc all round, join with Sl st to first ch.

NOTE Rnds 6 and 7 are turning rounds, which will create an edge, changing working from base to wall of pot.

Rnd 6 Ch 1, work evenly in Sl st all round, join with Sl st to first ch.

Rnd 7 Ch 1, work in Sl st all round, working into the back loop only of each Sl st on previous rnd, join with Sl st to first ch.

Rnds 8–14 Ch 1, work evenly in sc, with hook through whole st, all round, join with Sl st to first ch. Fasten off at end of rnd 14.

small pot lid

NOTE Work with A and B held together throughout.

Rnds 1–4 Rep rnds 1–4 of small pot.

Rnd 5 Ch 1, 1 sc in first sc, 1 sc, 2 sc in next sc, ★ 2 sc, 2 sc in next sc, rep from ★ all round, join with Sl st to first ch—48 sts.

Rnd 6 Ch 1, work evenly in sc all round, join with Sl st to first ch.

Rnds 7 and 8 Turning rounds, as rnds 6 and 7 of small pot.

Rnds 9 and 10 (wall of lid) Ch 1, work evenly in sc, with hook through whole st, all round, join with Sl st to first ch. Fasten off at end of rnd 10.

TRIM

NOTE Work with two strands of B, held together, throughout.

Attach yarn to any sc on rnd 10 of small pot lid.

Rnd 1 Ch 1, work evenly in sc all round, join with Sl st to first ch.

Rnd 2 Ch 1, ★ 3 ch, skip 1 sc, 1 sc, rep from ★ all round, join with Sl st to first ch; fasten off.

HANDLE

NOTE Work with two strands of B, held together, throughout.

Insert the hook, from RS to WS, through the center of the lid and draw through a loop of yarn. Ch 10, join with Sl st to first ch, fasten off. Use the hook to draw the end of the yarn through to the WS of the lid. Knot ends together and trim off any excess.

style tip Alter the height of the sides of the pots to make small trays—try adding your own trim pattern around the rim.

Large pot

NOTE Work with A and B held together throughout.

Rnds 1–4 Rep rnds 1–4 of small pot.

Rnd 5 Ch 1, 1 sc in first sc, 1 sc, 2 sc in next sc, ★ 2 sc, 2 sc in next sc, rep from ★ all round, join with Sl st to first ch—48 sts.

Rnd 6 Ch 1, work evenly in sc all round, join with Sl st to first ch.

Rnd 7 Ch 1, 1 sc in first sc, 2 sc, 2 sc in next sc, ★ 3 sc, 2 sc in next sc, rep from ★ all round, join with Sl st to first ch—60 sts.

Rnd 8 Ch 1, work evenly in sc all round, join with Sl st to first ch.

Rnd 9 Ch 1, 1 sc in first sc, 3 sc, 2 sc in next sc, ★ 4 sc, 2 sc in next sc, rep from ★ all round, join with Sl st to first ch—72 sts.

Rnd 10 Ch 1, work evenly in sc all round, join with Sl st to first ch.

Rnd 11 Ch 1, 1 sc in first sc, 4 sc, 2 sc in next sc, ★ 5 sc, 2 sc in next sc, rep from ★ all round, join with Sl st to first ch—84 sts.

Rnd 12 Ch 1, work evenly in sc all round, join with Sl st to first ch.

Rnd 13 Ch 1, 1 sc in first sc, 5 sc, 2 sc in next sc, ★ 6 sc, 2 sc in next sc, rep from ★ all round, join with Sl st to first ch—96 sts.

Rnd 14 Ch 1, work evenly in sc all round, join with Sl st to first ch.

Rnds 15 and 16 Turning rounds, as rnds 6 and 7 of small pot.

Rnds 17–23 Ch 1, work evenly in sc, with hook through whole st, all round, join with Sl st to first ch. Fasten off at end of rnd 23.

large pot lid

NOTE Work with A and B held together throughout.

Rnds 1–14 Rep rnds 1–14 of large pot.

Rnd 15 Ch 1, 1 sc in first sc, 6 sc, 2 sc in next sc, ★ 7 sc, 2 sc in next sc, rep from ★ all round, join with Sl st to first ch—108 sts.

Rnds 16–17 Turning rounds, as rnds 6 and 7 of small pot.

Rnds 18–19 Ch 1, work evenly in sc, with hook through whole st, all around; join with Sl st to first ch. Fasten off at end of rnd 19.

finishing

TASSEL

With a tapestry needle and one strand each of A and B, work 12 x 3" (7.5 cm) loops into a st in the center of the lid. Holding the loops together in one hand, wrap yarn A 4 or 5 times around the base of the loops close to the lid, and knot to secure. Trim the end of the knotted yarn, and the tops of the loops, to make the tassel (as shown below).

wastepaper basket

This brightly striped wastepaper basket will brighten up your study or workroom.

The design works up quickly using natural twine, which helps to keep the shape.

The beads are added as you go to make for simple embellishments—choose wooden or seedpod beads to suit the natural finish.

FINISHED MEASUREMENTS
- Height approx. 10" (25.5 cm)

MATERIALS
- 1 x 1 lb. (450 g) ball natural garden twine (MC)
- 1 x 5 oz. (140 g) ball dyed jute twine in each color of red (A), dark orange (B) and light orange (C)
- Size J-10 (6 mm) crochet hook OR SIZE NECESSARY TO OBTAIN CORRECT GAUGE
- Tapestry needle
- Stitch marker
- 84 assorted large eyed wooden beads in natural, pink, orange, and red. Make sure that the beads you choose will slide along the twine easily.

GAUGE
Base = 9½" (24 cm) diameter.
NOTE Gauge may vary, due to the varying thickness of the jute twine. Be sure to keep the stitches at an even tension throughout.

Wastepaper basket

base
Using MC, ch 5, join with a Sl st to form ring.
Rnd 1 Sc twice into every st, and place marker at the joining.
Rnd 2 Sc in every st.
Rnd 3 Inc every other st by sc twice into every 2nd st.
Rnd 4 Rep row 2.
Rnd 5 Inc every 3rd stitch.
Rnd 6 Rep row 3.
Rnd 7 Inc every 4th st.
Inc in this set pattern so the base enlarges evenly. Cont until base measures 9½" (24 cm) across. Place marker at the finishing point.

sides
NOTE Read before beg to crochet.
Sc into every st around the edge.
Turn the work so that the crochet hook faces you and work in the opposite direction. Make 5 rnds in sc and cut yarn, leaving a long end.
Cont sides using sc, foll the color pat below. For the bead rows, thread 12 beads in alt colors onto the twine before beg the rnds, then work a bead into every 6th st by sliding a bead down and making 1 sc behind it.
Work 3 rows with A—bead the 2nd row.
Next row Worked in C.
Next row Worked in MC.

Next row Work in B—bead row.

Next row Work in MC.

Next row Work in C.

Next row Work 3 rows with A—bead the 2nd rnd.

Next row Work 3 rows with MC.

Rep until sides measure 10" (25.5 cm).

finishing

Work Sl st in each st around top edge. Fasten off.

how to get started

The basics of crochet are very simple—even the most complicated and decorative stitches are just variations on a simple chain. These instructions are all for a right-handed person. If you are left-handed, look at the pictures in a mirror and they should show you the correct way to do the stitch.

holding the hook and yarn

To crochet successfully it is important to hold the yarn and hook in a correct and comfortable manner. This will ensure that the gauge is accurate and consistent throughout your chosen project. There are many ways of holding the hook and yarn in crochet, and it may feel awkward at first. Here are just two examples—choose whichever variation seems to come most naturally to you.

holding the hook

Try holding the hook in your right hand as you would a knife.

Alternatively, hold the hook in your right hand as you would a pencil.

holding the yarn

Some crocheters like to wrap the ball end of the yarn around the little finger of the left hand, passing it under the third and middle finger, and over the forefinger, using the forefinger to control the tension.

Also try wrapping the ball end of the yarn around the little finger of your left hand, passing it over the other 3 fingers. Hold work steady with your thumb and forefinger; use the middle finger to create tension.

measuring gauge

Before starting on a project, you must do a gauge swatch to ensure that you are crocheting with the same gauge as the pattern. If you work a pattern in the wrong gauge it will not have the correct finished measurements. The swatch should be just over 4" (10 cm) square using the same stitch that is used in the pattern, or as indicated by the instructions. Knitter's pins are useful as the large heads won't disappear through the holes in the fabric.

1 Measure out 4" (10 cm) across the width of your swatch, using one of the rows as a guide. Place markers.

2 Measure out 4" (10 cm) down the length of the swatch (across the rows). Place markers. Use these two sets of markers to count how many stitches and rows there are to 4" (10 cm), and compare to the gauge given at the start of your pattern.

. . . .

make a slipknot

In order to begin crocheting and make your first chain, you will need to make a slipknot.

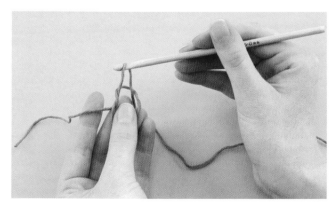

1 Make a loop in the yarn. With your crochet hook, catch the ball end of the yarn and draw it through the loop as shown.

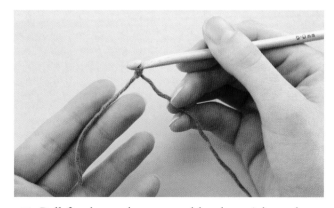

2 Pull firmly on the yarn and hook to tighten the knot and create the first loop.

making a chain

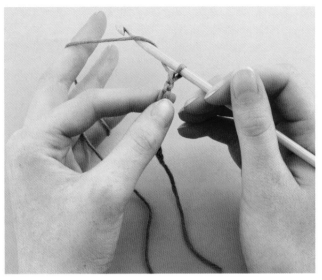

1 To make a chain, hold the tail end of the yarn with the left hand and bring the yarn over hook (yoh) by passing hook in front of the yarn, under and around it.

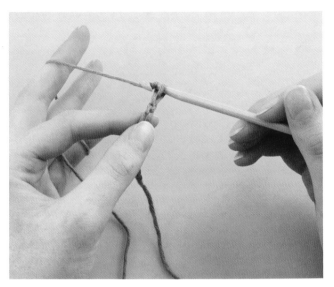

2 Keeping the tension in the yarn taut, draw the hook and yarn through the loop.

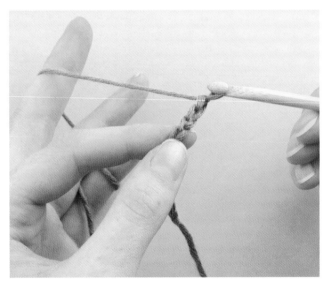

3 Pull the yarn and hook through the hole and begin again, ensuring that the stitches are fairly loose. Repeat to make the number of stitches required. As the chain lengthens, keep hold of the bottom edge to maintain the tension.

how to count a chain To count the stitches, use the right side of the chain, or the side that has more visible and less twisted V shapes, as shown below. Don't count the original slip stitch, but count each V as 1 chain. There are 8 stitches on this chain.

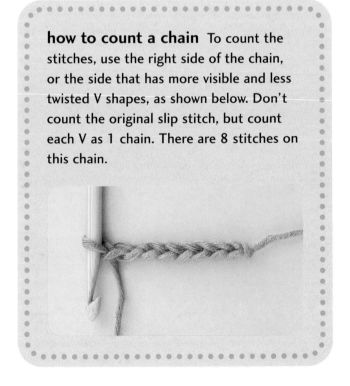

make a slip stitch (Sl st)

A slip stitch is used to join one stitch to another, as in joining a circle, or a stitch to another point, and is usually made by picking up two strands of a stitch. However, where it is worked into the starting chain only pick up the back loop, as shown here.

1 Insert the hook into the back loop of the next stitch and pass the yarn over the hook (yoh), as in chain stitch.

2 Draw the yarn through both loops on the stitch, and repeat.

what to do at the end of a row

At the end of a row, when you turn the work to begin the next, you need to complete a turning chain to get to the right height of the stitch you are working. This chain counts as the first stitch in the row, and each technique, depending on its height, uses a different number of chain stitches at the start of the row.

After completing a row, turn work. Make turning chain in the same way as a normal chain. Yoh. Draw yarn through loop on hook and repeat to height of chain required (see table below).

turning chain table

TYPE OF STITCH	CHAIN STITCHES
single crochet	1
half double crochet	2
double crochet	3
treble crochet	4
double treble	5

Single crochet (sc) Here you can see that the hook is passed through the whole stitch (two loops), before the yarn is drawn back through the loops to complete the stitch.

1 Insert hook, front to back into next stitch, 2 strands and 1 loop on hook. Yoh.

2 Draw through to front, 2 loops on hook.

3 Yoh.

4 Draw through both loops to complete sc. Work 1 sc into every stitch to end.

Half double crochet (hdc) This is a popular stitch that makes a firm fabric.
The yarn is drawn through three loops to make the stitch.

1 Yoh.

2 Insert hook in next stitch, from front to back and draw through the stitch only.

3 This creates 3 loops on the hook.

4 Yoh and draw yarn through 3 remaining loops on hook together to complete hdc.

Double crochet (dc) This makes a more open fabric. The stitch is confusingly called a "treble" in the UK because of the three moves it takes to make the stitch.

1 Wrap the yarn over the hook (yoh) from back to front, so there are 2 loops on the hook.

2 Insert hook in next stitch, from front to back. Yoh and draw through stitch.

3 You will now have 3 loops on hook. Yoh and pull through 2 loops.

4 Now there are 2 loops on hook. Yoh.

5 Pull through remaining 2 loops to complete dc.

Treble crochet (tr)

You will need a turning chain of four to reach the height of this elongated stitch, as shown on the turning chain table on page 93.

1 Wrap yarn round hook twice (yoh twice).

2 Insert hook into next stitch, yoh.

3 Pull yarn through stitch to front, 4 loops on hook, yoh.

4 Draw yarn through 2 loops, leaving 3 loops on the hook. Yoh again.

5 Draw yarn through 2 loops, leaving 2 loops on hook, yoh.

6 Pull yarn through both remaining loops to complete a treble stitch (tr).

Double treble (dtr) This stitch combines a double and a treble together to make a fabric with tall posts. You will need a five loop turning chain when working this stitch.

1 Wind yarn round hook 3 times (yoh 3 times).

2 Insert hook into next stitch, yoh, and pull through stitch to front.

3 Now you have 5 loops on hook, yoh and pull through 2 loops.

4 Now with 4 loops on hook, yoh and pull through 2 loops.

5 With 3 loops on hook, yoh and pull through 2 loops.

6 Now with 2 loops on hook, yoh and pull through all remaining loops on hook.

Working in the round
There are two ways to begin circular crochet, using either a chain or a loop. The loop method ensures no hole is formed in the middle of your work.

making a chain ring

1 Work a chain as long as required by pattern.

2 Join last chain to first with a slip stitch. Begin first round by working into each chain stitch.

making a yarn loop

This way of working in the round ensures that there is no hole in the middle of the work, as there is with a chain ring.

1 Make a loop with tail end of yarn on right, ball end on left.

2 Pull ball end through loop (you will need to steady work with hand).

3 Make 1 chain through loop on hook you have drawn through to steady the round.

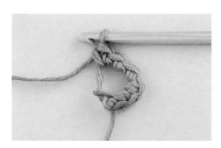

4 Work as many sc, or whatever stitch you are using, into the loop as required by pattern.

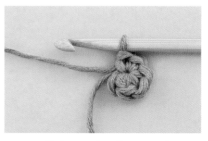

5 Pull the ends of yarn tight to draw in circle—no hole in the middle of first round.

Circular crochet

Working in rounds as opposed to rows means the last stitch of each round is joined by a slip stitch to the first stitch, and the work continues as such, round and round, with no turning. This means it is easy to lose which row you are on—stitch markers will remind you of where you started. To create a flat circle rather than a tube, you will need to increase in every row. Work two stitches into each chain in the first row, then every other stitch in the following row, every third stitch in the third row, and so on. At the beginning of each round it is still necessary to make the turning chain, even though you are not actually turning the work—unless you are just going round in a spiral, which creates a less even shape.

1 To join a new color, fasten off first color and make a slipknot on your hook. Insert hook from front to back in stitch where you wish to begin new color. Draw the hook through to front.

2 Make chain to get work to height of stitch used.

3 Insert hook into next stitch and work stitch required by pattern.

4 Continue to work round until you reach the beginning of round, (marked with a stitch marker). Join round with Sl st to top of first chain.

Afghan squares

"Granny" squares can be worked quickly, and form the basis of many designs in this book, where they are joined together to make a bigger shape. They can be stitched in one color, or in many colors, making them a great way to use up oddments of yarn.

1 Make 5 chain, Sl st in first ch to join circle. Work into circle, 3 ch to count as first dc. 2 dc in circle. ★ 2 ch, 3 dc. Repeat from ★ twice more. Join with Sl st to 3 ch at beginning of round. Chain 5—first 3 are dc, last 2, sp.

2 3 dc, 2 ch, 3 dc into first 2 ch space of previous row. This forms corner. ★ 1 ch [3 dc, 2 ch, 3 dc] into next 2-ch sp. Repeat from ★ twice more. Join with Sl st to top of first chain.

3 The pattern progresses with each row. For next rows, cont as step 2, using instructions in parentheses for corners, and [1 ch, 3 dc] into sp in middle of rows.

alternative motif Make a number of variations to the basic square. These will allow you to personalize any afghan square project in the book.

Cluster stitches These are made up of groups of stitches that are only half finished, worked into the same space, and then joined together. The number of stitches worked will vary between stitches and patterns.

bobbles (bo)

When working this stitch on every row, put at least 1 dc between each bobble. You can also experiment, by varying how many dc you work into same space.

1 After last dc, dc into next stitch, but don't do last draw through, which means you will have 2 loops on hook. For example; yoh, insert hook into stitch, draw through stitch, yoh, draw through 2 loops. Leave last 2 loops on hook. Repeat this half closed dc 4 more times into the same space. 6 loops on hook. Yoh.

2 Draw yarn through all 6 loops on hook. Bobble made—it will have a raised, spherical look.

finished bobbles Make a sample before including this stitch in a pattern.

popcorns (pc)

When working this stitch on every row put at least 1 dc between each popcorn. The stitch is similar to a bobble, but is slanted. You may also experiment by varying how many dc you work into same space.

1 After dc, work 5 dc into the next stitch.

2 Remove hook from loop and insert from front to back into first dc in space and back through original loop. Yoh, draw yarn through all loops on hook. Popcorn completed.

finished popcorns If you want the popcorn to slant in the opposite direction, replace the removed needle from back to front and then through original loop, yoh, draw through. Work a sample square before including in a pattern for the first time.

puffs

When working this stitch, in each row, put at least 1 dc between each puff. You can also experiment by varying how many loops you work into the same space.

1 Yoh and draw large loop through very loosely. Repeat 5 more times into same stitch—7 loops on hook.

2 Yoh and pull through 6 loops, leaving original on hook. 2 loops on hook. Yoh and pull through remaining loops. Puff complete.

finished puffs Work a sample square before including this stitch in a pattern. Textured stitches are a great way to personalize a design, but can take some getting used to.

shells

Alternate the shell clusters with single crochet along each row. To create the half–drop shell repeat shown in this picture, begin first row with a sc and second row with a shell cluster, and repeat these rows throughout.

1 Work 5 dc into next stitch. Shell cluster made.

2 Work 1 sc into following stitch and continue in this way along the row.

3 Cont in pattern to make fabric square with scalloped edge.

alternative shell fabric To personalize a design using shell pattern, experiment to create your own texture.

Embroidery

An effective way of adding interest to your projects, embroidery complements the texture of the crochet. Here are some simple stitches that you may like to try. Use a blunt, tapestry needle to work the stitches, as this will not split the yarn of the crocheted fabric as embroidery needles do, and will slip between the crochet stitches easily.

chain stitch

Insert needle from back to front of work and loop the thread back into same hole from front to back. Bring the needle back through to the front 1 stitch length away and catch the loop with the point of the needle to create a chain. This is a useful stitch for curved shapes like flowers, or for handwriting script.

blanket stitch

This stitch creates a neat edge, and is useful for straightening an uneven selvage. Working along the edge, secure yarn at the back of work, insert the needle from front to back, with needle coming out of work in front of loop made by yarn. Pull needle through, tightening yarn against edge of work; repeat for length of edge.

satin stitch

Work stitches closely together along the shape of the pattern you wish to make, keeping edges of shape even. This is most commonly used as a color filler for petals and other solid shapes.

Edgings
One of the best ways to employ crochet is to produce neat and decorative edgings. These designs need not be restricted to crochet fabrics; they look just as interesting on knitted or loosely woven fabrics, and can be used to personalize your finished garments.

reverse sc (corded) edging
Join yarn to edge of work. Begin by working 1 row of sc evenly along the edge of work, being careful not to pull the stitch too tight. Next, work back along the row in sc, without turning work, from left to right.

shell edging
Join yarn to edge of work. Begin by working 1 row of sc evenly along the edge of work, being careful not to pull the work too tightly. Turn. Next, work a Sl st into first stitch, ★ miss 2 sts, 5 dc into next stitch, miss 2 sts, Sl st into next stitch. Rep from ★ for length of edge.

picot edging
Use either with or without foundation row of sc (this sample has the foundation row). Work 1 sc into each of the first 3 stitches. ★ 4 ch, remove hook from last ch and insert in first of 4-ch, pick up ch just dropped and draw through loop on hook to create picot, 1 sc into each of next 3 sts. Rep from ★ to end.

Finishing off
The final steps are a very important part of crochet, as it will make or break your work. The perfect join will be indistinguishable from the crochet—bad finishing is always noticeable, and will make the whole project look messy.

fastening off

1 After finishing the last stitch, snip off yarn from ball, leaving a short length to weave in. Yoh.

2 Draw through tail, pulling tightly to fasten.

• •

weaving in ends

1 Use hook to draw yarn through at least 5 stitches, winding the yarn over and under as you go to secure yarn and ensure it doesn't work free.

2 Snip off excess yarn. Always weave in ends securely, otherwise they will work free, and could begin to unravel.

Joining work

slip stitch join

Place the pieces together, right sides facing. Work a row of Sl st along the join, inserting needle through back loops only of both pieces (the 2 loops which touch when placed side by side).

single crochet join

Place the pieces together, right sides facing. Work a row of sc along the join of both pieces, going through the whole of both stitches.

whipstitch

Place the pieces together, right sides facing. Using a tapestry needle, join the back loops of each piece with a diagonal stitch.

Useful information

Wouldn't it be great if everyone used the same terms to write about yarns, and crochet hooks? Unfortunately, sizes are often based on metric or imperial measurements, or use arbitrary systems of numbers and letters. If in doubt, use a needle gauge to find the millimeter measurement of your crochet hooks.

On these pages you will find some conversion charts that will help you to convert hooks and yarns into the standard sizes that are used in the patterns. These charts are based on the recommendations of the Craft Yarn Council of America. You can see further information on their website, www.yarnstandards.com.

yarn weights

If you are going to use a different fiber than the one recommended, it is crucial that you do a gauge swatch to ensure that you can match the gauge given at the beginning of each pattern, otherwise your work will not match the finished measurements supplied.

Use the chart below as a guide to help find the right gauge for your new wool, and to choose which weight of yarn to buy to match the symbol given with each pattern.

YARN WEIGHT SYMBOL GIVEN IN THE PATTERN	1	2	3	4	5	6
TYPES OF YARNS IN CATEGORY	Sock, fingering, baby	Sport, baby	Double knitting, light worsted	Worsted, afghan, Aran	Chunky, craft, rug	Bulky, roving
CROCHET GAUGE IN SINGLE CROCHET TO 4" (10 CM)	21–32 sts	16–20 sts	12–17 sts	11–14 sts	8–11 sts	5–9 sts
RECOMMENDED HOOK IN METRIC RANGE	2.25–3.5 mm	3.5–4.5 mm	4.5–5.5 mm	5.5–6.5 mm	6.5–9 mm	9 mm and larger
RECOMMENDED HOOK RANGE	B-1 to E-4	E-4 to 7	7 to I-9	I-9 to K-10½	K-10½ to M/N-13	M/N-13 and larger

CROCHET HOOK SIZES

USA Size	Millimeters (mm)
B-1	2.25
C-2	2.75
D-3	3.25
E-4	3.5
F-5	3.75
G-6	4
7	4.5
H-8	5
I-9	5.5
J-10	6
K-10½	6.5
L-11	8
M/N-13	9
N/P-15	10
P/Q	15
Q	16
S	19

abbreviations

Looking at a crochet pattern for the first time must feel like reading another language. The shortened words are really there to prevent laborious repetition, and of course, to make the patterns shorter and easier to follow. Any special or unusual abbreviations used in the book are mentioned at the start of the pattern. These are the main ones that you will encounter in this book.

[ ]	work instructions within brackets as many times as directed
( )	work instructions within parentheses as many times as directed
★	repeat the instructions following the single asterisk as directed
★★	repeat instructions between asterisks as many times as directed or repeat from a given set of instructions
A, B, D	color A, color B, color D and so on
alt	alternate
approx	approximately
beg	begin/beginning
bet	between
bl	back loop(s)
bo	bobble
BP	back post
BPdc	back post double crochet
BPsc	back post single crochet
BPtr	back post treble crochet
CC	contrasting color
ch	chain stitch

ch-	refers to chain or space previously made: e.g., ch-1 space
ch-sp	chain space
CL	cluster
cm	centimeter(s)
cont	continue
dc	double crochet
dc2tog	double crochet 2 stitches together
dec	decrease/decreases/decreasing
dtr	double treble
fL	front loop(s)
foll	follow/follows/following
FP	front post
FPdc	front post double crochet
FPsc	front post single crochet
FPtr	front post treble crochet
g	gram
hdc	half double crochet
hdc2tog	half double crochet 2 stitches together
inc	increase(s)/increasing
lp(s)	loops
m	meter(s)
MC	main color
mm	millimeter(s)

oz	ounce(s)
p	picot
pat(s)	pattern(s)
pc	popcorn
pm	place marker
prev	previous
rem	remain/remaining
rep	repeat(s)
rnd(s)	round(s)
RS	right side
sc	single crochet
sc2tog	single crochet 2 stitches together
sk	skip
Sl st	slip stitch
sp(s)	space(s)
st(s)	stitch(es)
tch or t-ch	turning chain
tbl	through back loop
tog	together
tr	treble crochet
trtr	triple treble crochet
WS	wrong side
yd(s)	yard(s)
yo	yarn over
yoh	yarn over hook

Acknowledgments

Many, many thanks to Joyce Nordstrom, and her talented team of crocheters, and to Annette Breindel, Gayle Bunn, and Bibi Wein.

Thanks also to the following designers:

Lucinda Ganderton
Pearly Napkin Rings

Karin Hossack
Wastepaper Basket

Ruth Maddock
Floral Tiebacks

Claire Montgomerie
Dresser-top Pots, Table Centerpiece, and Album Cover

Sources for supplies

Contact the companies listed below for purchasing and mail-order information.

yarn

Blue Sky Alpacas
PO Box 387, St. Francis, MN 55070
www.blueskyalpacas.com

Cascade Yarns
1224 Andover Park East, Tukwila, WA 98188
www.cascadeyarns.com

Coats & Clark/TLC/J&P Coats
PO Box 12229, Greenville, SC 29612-0229
www.coatsandclark.com

DMC
The DMC Corporation
South Hackensack Avenue
Port Kearny Bldg. 10F, South Kearny, NJ 07032-4688
www.dmc-usa.com

GGH
Distributed by Muench Yarns
1323 Scott Street Petaluma, CA 94954
www.muenchyarns.com

Lion Brand Yarn
135 Kero Road, Carlstadt, NJ 07072
www.lionbrand.com

Lousa Harding Yarns
www.louisaharding.co.uk

Patons Yarns
320 Livingstone Avenue South, Listowel, ON, Canada, N4W 3H3
www.patonsyarns.com

Rowan Yarns/Westminster Fibers
4 Townsend West, Unit 8, Nashua, NH 03063
www.knitrowan.com

Tahki/Stacy Charles
70–30 80th St., Building 36, Ridgewood, NY 11385
www.tahkistacycharles.com